AI DREAMING: PALINDROMES

CLASSIC WORDPLAY ILLUSTRATED WITH MIDJOURNEY AI

JAMES LAWSON

Fiddlehead Press

Art (interior and cover) created using Midjourney AI, prompted/iterated/curated by James Lawson

ISBN: 9781680131550 (Paperback)
ISBN: 9781680131567 (Ebook)
ISBN: 9781680131574 (Hardcover)

Subjects: Art/Digital; Computers/Design, Graphics & Media/General; Computers/Artificial Intelligence

Fiddlehead Press
Olympia, WA
anthea@anthealawson.com

Fiddlehead Press

INTRODUCTION

It is rare moment when amateur artists and non-artists can participate in a watershed moment in art history. That time is now.

Welcome to the wild frontier of AI image generation. Rapidly advancing machine learning systems with names like DALL-E, Imagen, Midjourney, and Stable Diffusion are just now becoming available to the public. The images they create are astounding.

Taking just simple text prompts from the user, these systems are capable of generating sophisticated images in a wide variety of artistic styles. Can you imagine a dog paddling a canoe? A map of a city in the style of Leonardo Da Vinci? A winter scene in the suburbs? An alien alphabet? If so, you can use one of these systems to bring that vision to life.

The results won't always match your imagination. In fact, the images seldom do, and there will be many surprises and chose classic palindrome sentences to use as prompts for the AI. Sometimes, I would add the name of an artist, person, or an art medium (such as charcoal or oil paints) to get more varied artistic styles.

From the initial prompts, I would have the AI generate many different output images. Often I would run the prompt over and over, generating hundreds of images. From these I selected the best three to illustrate the palindrome.

The images in this book are all output straight from the AI. I didn't modify them in Photoshop or any other program.

After using Midjourney AI intensively, I'm convinced this type of image generation is a game changer. Like the invention of photography, it will allow the masses to create and enjoy images. It will disrupt things, and it will open new doors undreamed of. A few people of exceptional talent and skill will use this technology to create the art of their generation.

PALINDROME 101

What's a palindrome? A palindrome is simply a fancy name for a word, phrase, or sequence that reads the same forward and back.

For example, "nurses run" is a palindrome. So is "Wow" and the number "101."

The word "palindrome," unfortunately, is not one. I think that is a grave error. My feelings about that omission can, however, be described by the palindrome, "Dammit, I'm mad!"

According to the official rules, punctuation and spaces aren't counted when determining palindromes. Therefore, "Naomi, did I moan?" counts even though it doesn't have two matching commas and two question marks in the sequence.

The best palindromes make some kind of bizarre sense. They are compressed nuggets of literary surrealism that tell a little story and make you laugh with their weirdness. Things like, "No sir, away! A papaya war is on!" Who wouldn't want

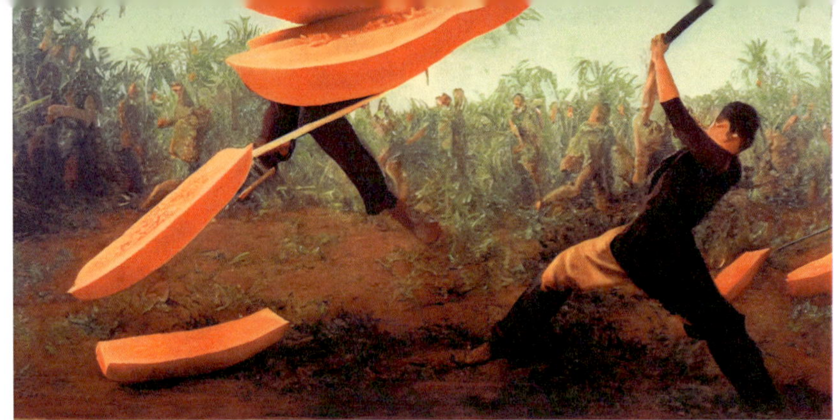

No Sir, away! A papaya war is on!

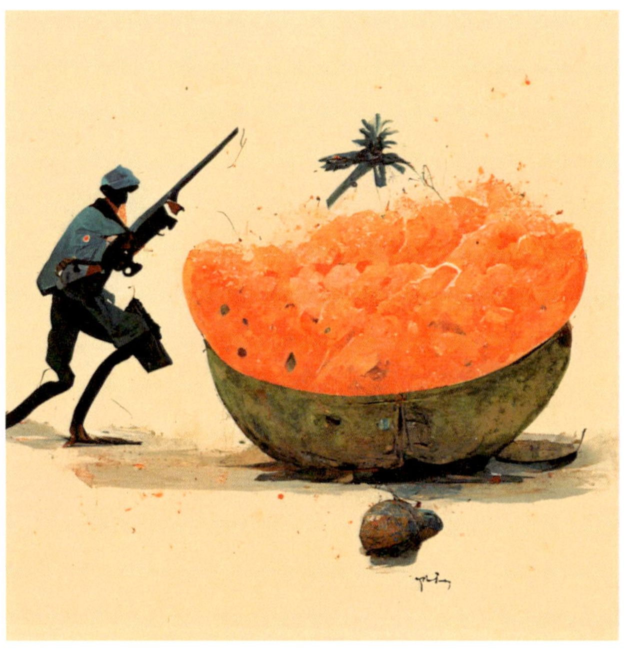

HOW THE IMAGES WERE MADE

Working with an AI image generation system like Midjourney is a completely different way of making images. There are no pencils, or markers. No canvases or spilled paints.

The process is textual, conceptual, interactive and surprising. Image generation starts with a typed prompt. You try one approach, then another. You study the names of art styles and gemstones and architects to develop your own artistic vocabulary. You work with the limitations of a developing technology (and abandon any hope of getting realistic-looking hands). You become an AI whisperer.

Although the process feels like magic, it is definitely a collaboration. It's more like riding a horse than driving a car. A car goes where you steer it; a horse, ultimately, goes where it agrees to go.

Every image in this book started as a text prompt to the Midjourney GAI. The words provide the inspiration. They nail form.

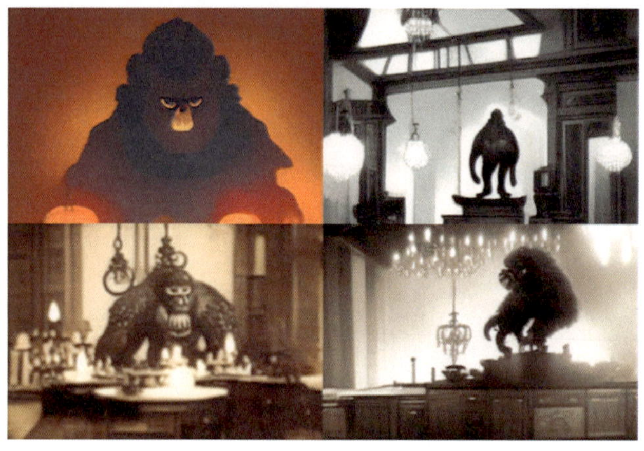

Midjourney Version 3 generates four thumbnails.

The system outputs a 4-grid of possible images. You can choose to upscale (enlarge and refine) any or all of them. If none of them suit, you can direct the AI to continue to make variations of any of the options, or even start from scratch to see what new images the system will generate.

This image nailed the "angry gorilla" idea, but ignored the "on the table" and "chandelier" prompts.

If none of the thumbnail ideas work, you can always rerun the prompt. I really wanted the gorilla on the table with a chandelier, so I kept going, found an output image I liked, and asked the AI to generate more variations of it.

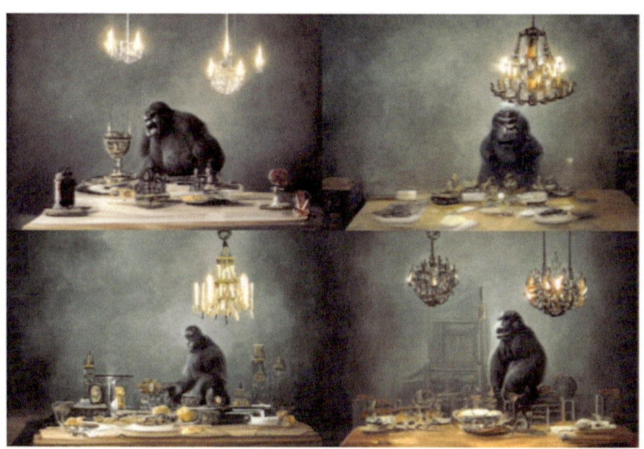

The AI generating related variations.

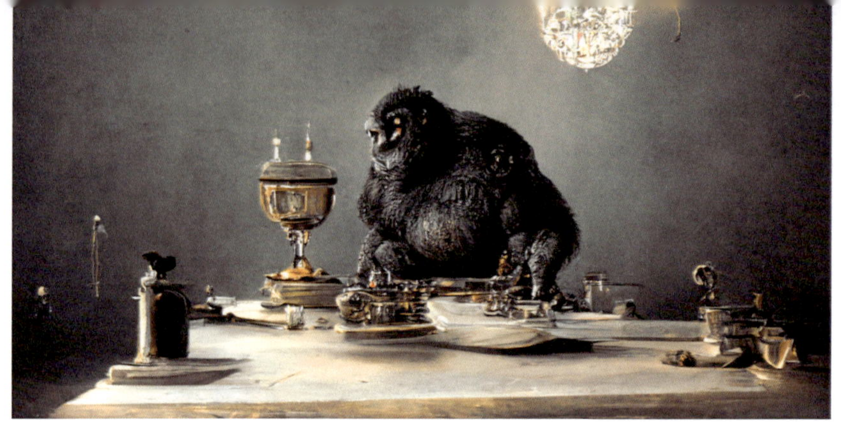

An angry gorilla standing on a kitchen table under a chandelier.

I liked the feel of this image, even though the gorilla's face was not very clear. He displays a simmering anger. He can't even bring himself to look at you. The AI went wild with chandeliers. It even added a floating lightbulb. That's to be expected. AI image systems are still in their infancy.

To give you an idea of how fast the technology is developing, here are images made after a Midjourney AI update, a couple weeks after the series above was finished. Using the very same prompt, here are examples of angry gorilla goodness from the improved AI:

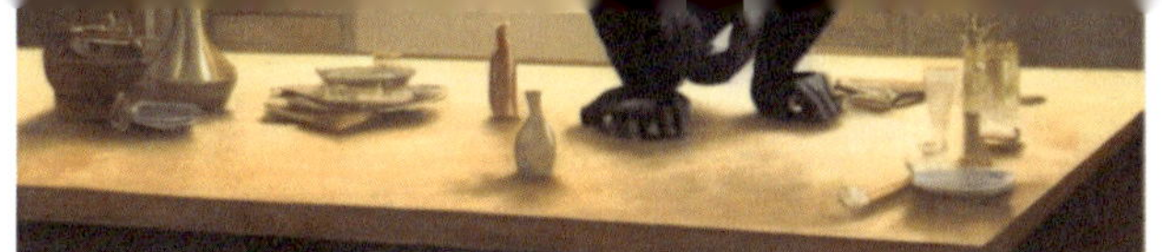

Same gorilla prompt, better gorilla drawing, especially the face.

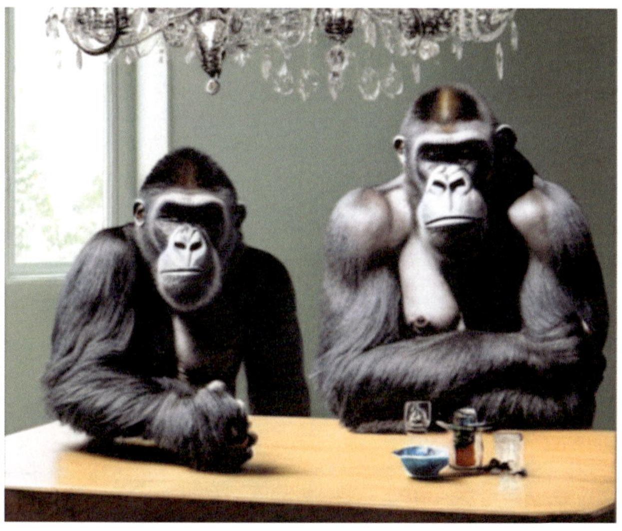

I guess the angry ape has an angry friend. Look at the body language the AI associates with the word Angry. Amazing!

Control of the final image is limited, so it's best to begin with a general idea rather than a very specific requirement.

THE PALINDROMES

TACO CAT

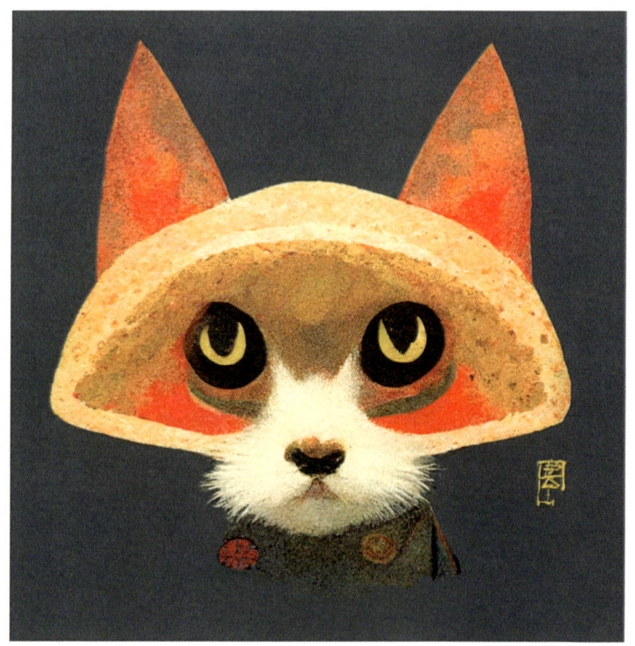

The internet loves Taco Cats. So does MidJourney AI. Part of its creativity comes from the ability to visually combine two objects that don't usually go together.

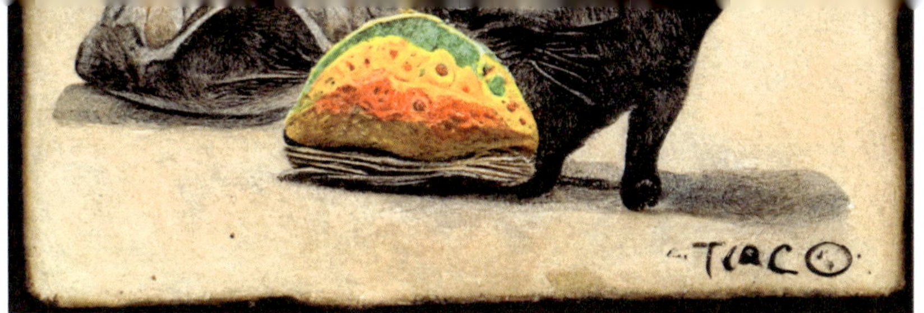

I added "cute" to the Taco Cat prompt when developing this image. Cute accomplished.

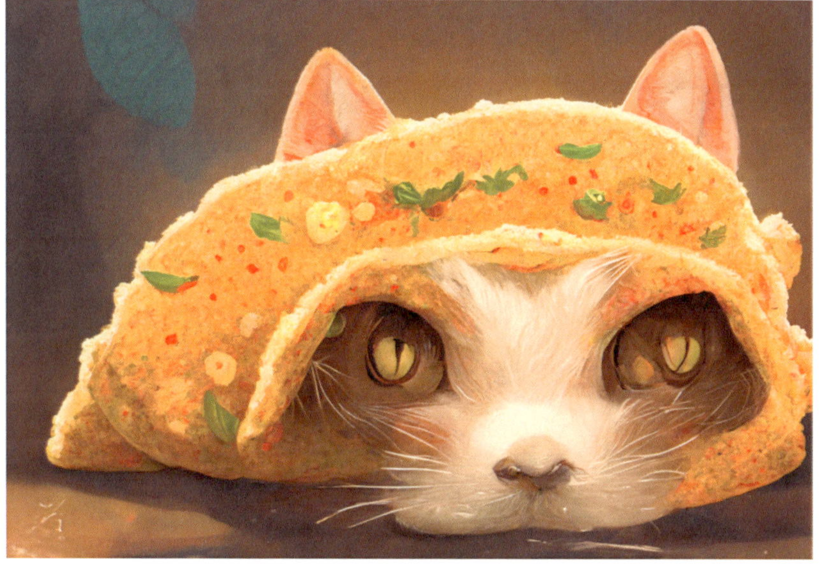

Crunchy cat. This is the image that started this whole palindrome book. Love those cat eyes and whiskers.

GOD, A RED NUGGET, A FAT EGG UNDER A DOG

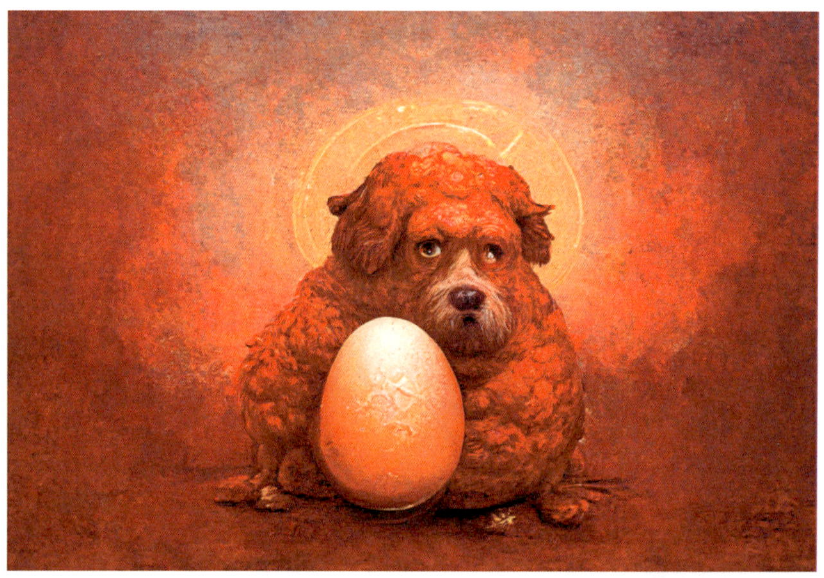

Midjourney AI responded to the palindrome prompt by generating this fat, saintly nugget dog cradling his favorite egg. I love the painterly halo illuminating the scene. Like any good painter, the AI has learned a lot about simulating light.

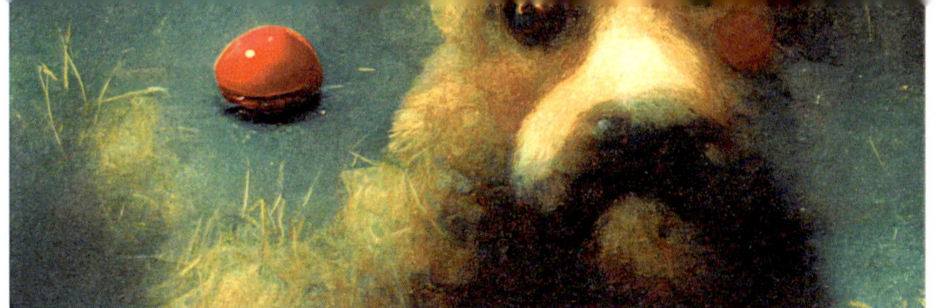

Here is a very different version developed from the same prompt. Is it the giant sky dog looking down from the heavens? Or maybe a reflection of a dog that has lost his favorite red egg in a still pond?

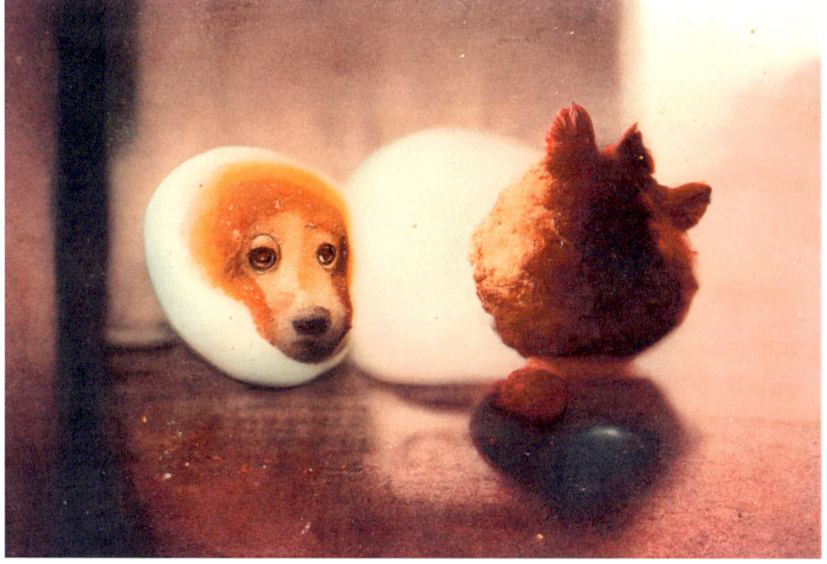

I never realized dogs hatch from eggs until I developed this work. AI-generated artwork often has a surreal quality.

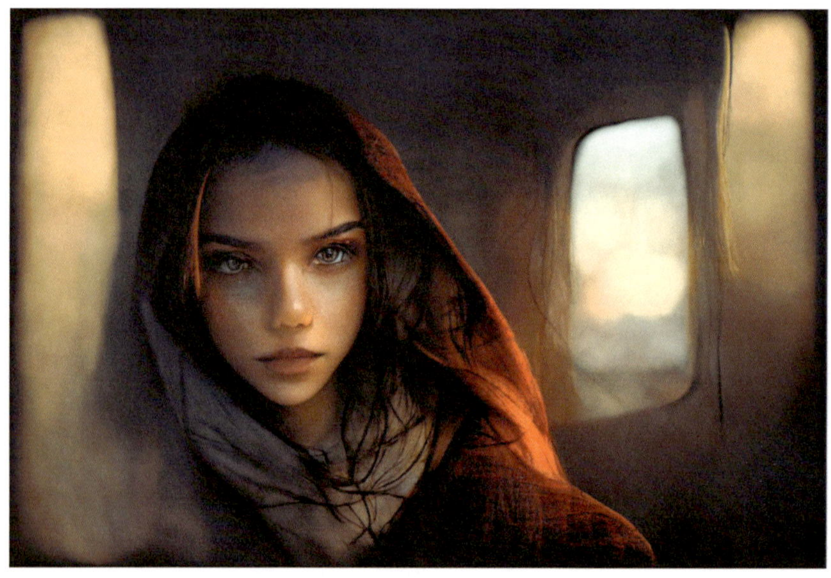

Midjourney AI Version 3 had trouble drawing noses and eyes. I developed about fifteen versions of this image that just couldn't be used. The eye and nose issues have mostly been fixed in recent updates to the system.

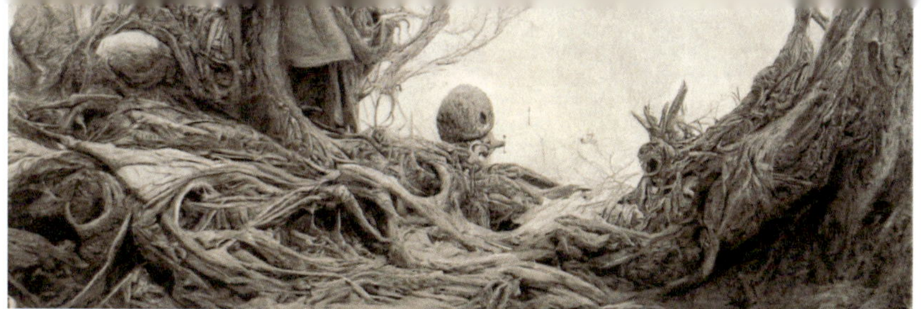

Another remote elf in a completely different style. I added "detailed ink drawing" to the prompt to nudge Midjourney to draw the image in that style.

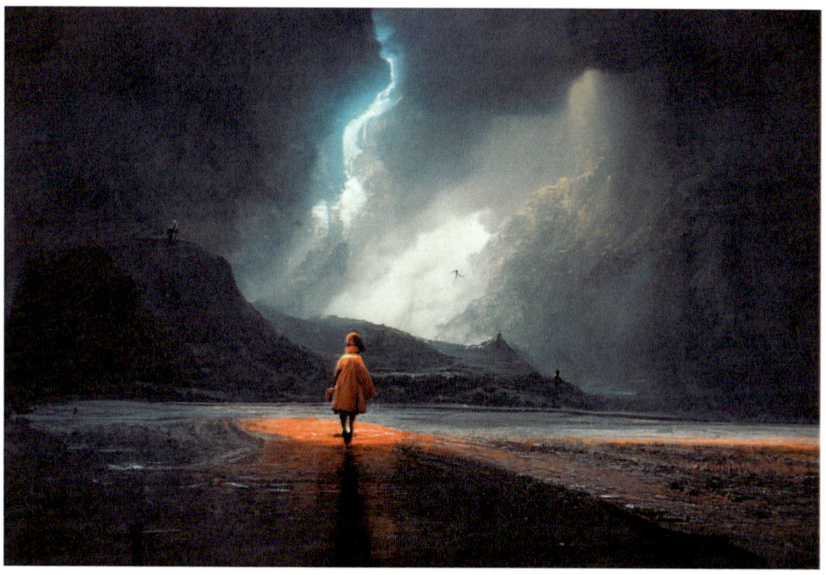

Another "Flee to me, remote elf." This time I asked Midjourney to create an image in a cinematic style with dramatic lighting.

A MAN, A PLAN, A CANAL, PANAMA

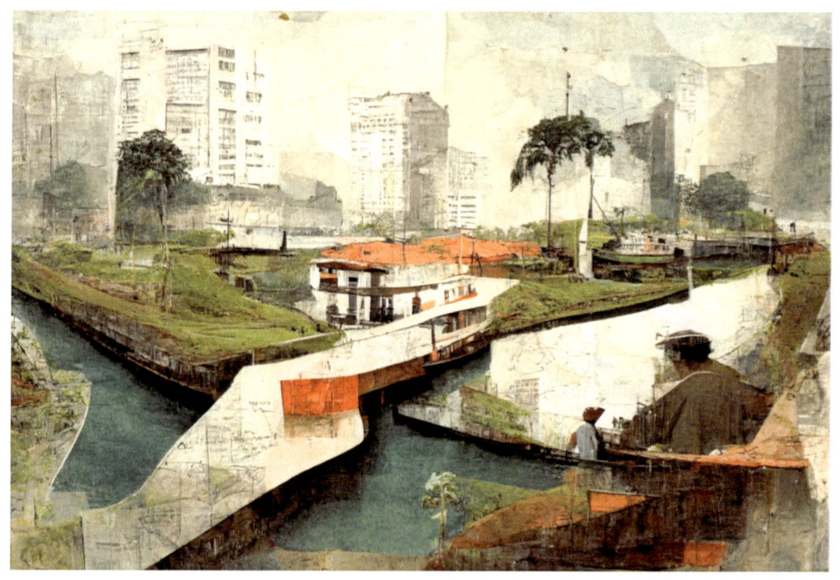

Midjourney's image inspired by a palindrome classic about the building of the Panama canal. I specified "in the style of a collage" for this series.

I added “Teddy Roosevelt” to the prompt. Specifying a person or character inspires the AI to face the character forward; otherwise it often defaults to a figure looking away. Discovering these kinds of tricks is part of the fun.

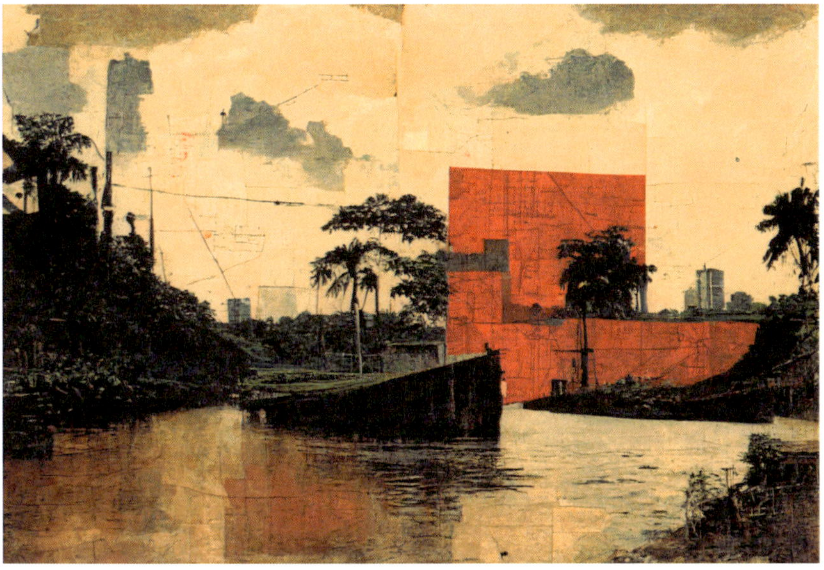

A final Panama Canal image. It’s amazing that Midjourney gets palm trees and ships, Panama City, and painterly reflections on the water from such a simple prompt.

A CAR, A MAN, A MARACA

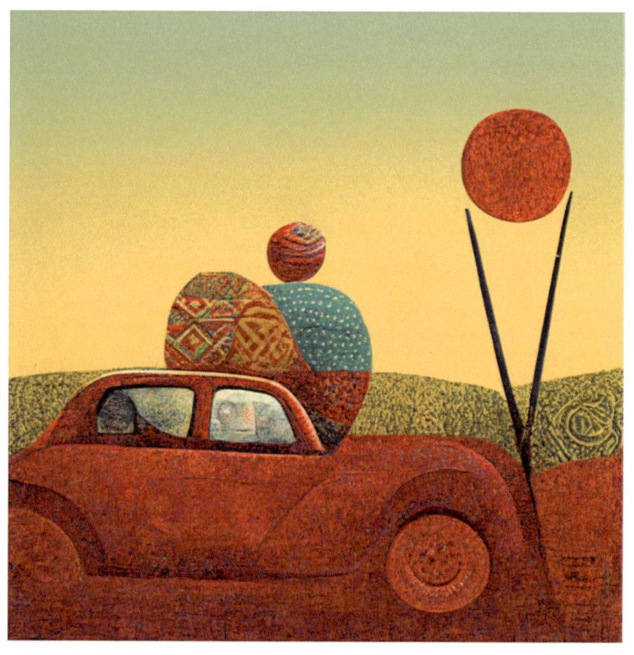

I thought Midjourney would have no problem with this prompt, but it actually took a lot of tinkering to get images that worked. I added fabric to the prompt for this image.

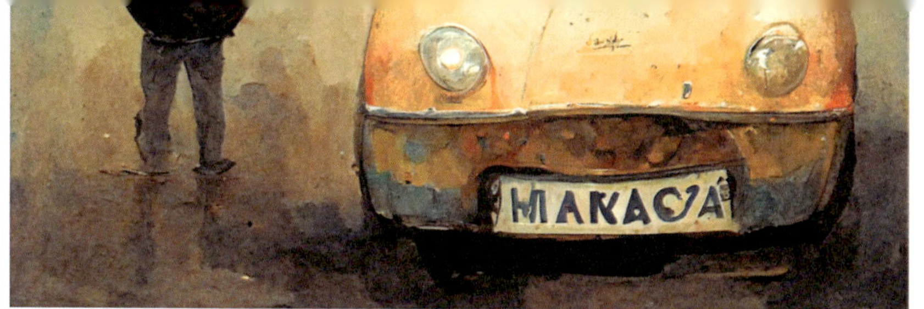

Man as a Maraca. Notice MidJourney trying to put the prompt word “Maraca” on the car license plate.

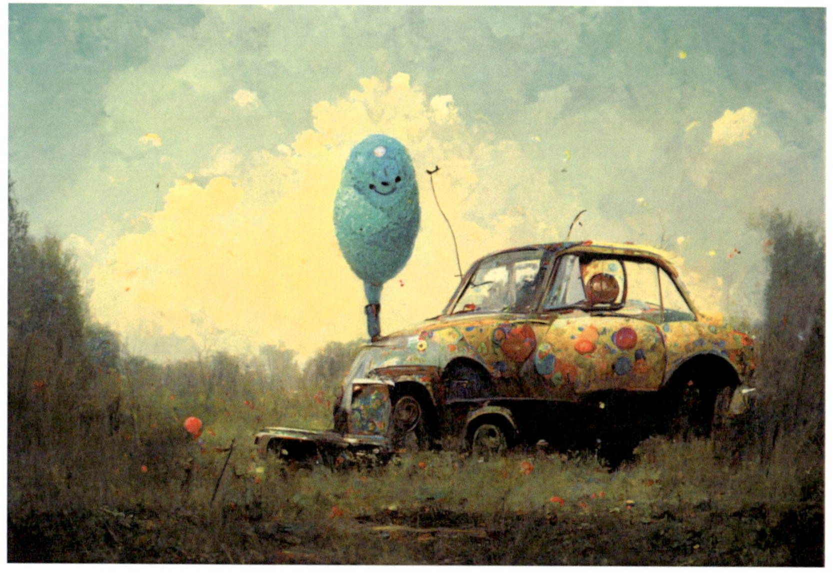

Something about the word Maraca added a lot of color to the images. I don’t know where the little happy face on the Maraca came from.

ABBA

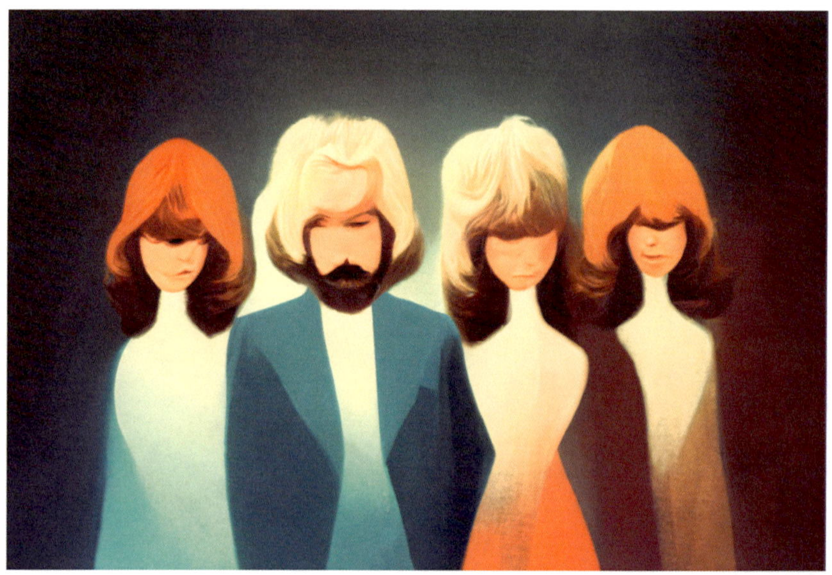

The 70's supergroup whose name is a palindrome formed from the members' initials. I included "1970's" in the prompt for this image. Dig those hair styles and warm, earthy tones.

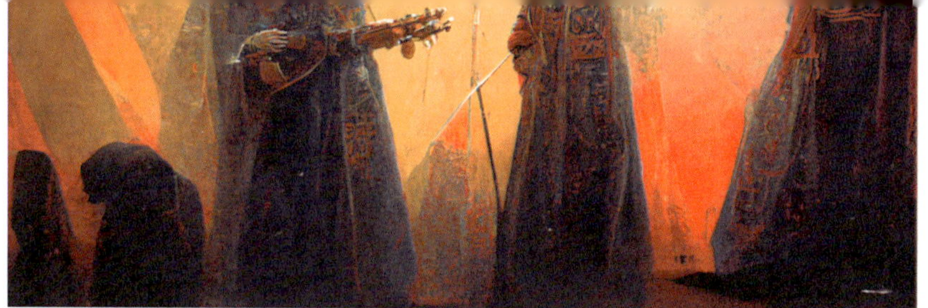

This is MidJourney's vision of an ABBA concert. The AI kept putting the band in traditional garb. I understand that Abba means "father" in Hebrew and Arabic.

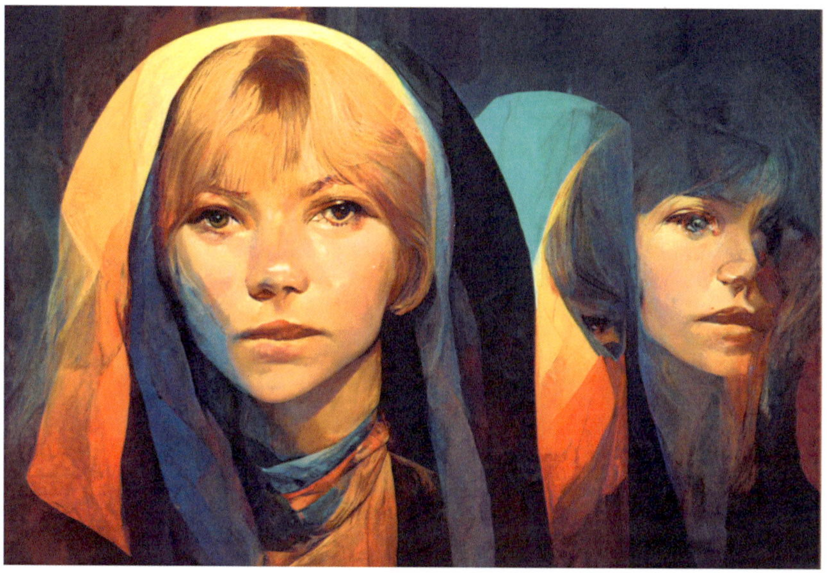

I love the faces and colors on this one. Another satisfying and unexpected image.

ACROBAT STAB ORCA

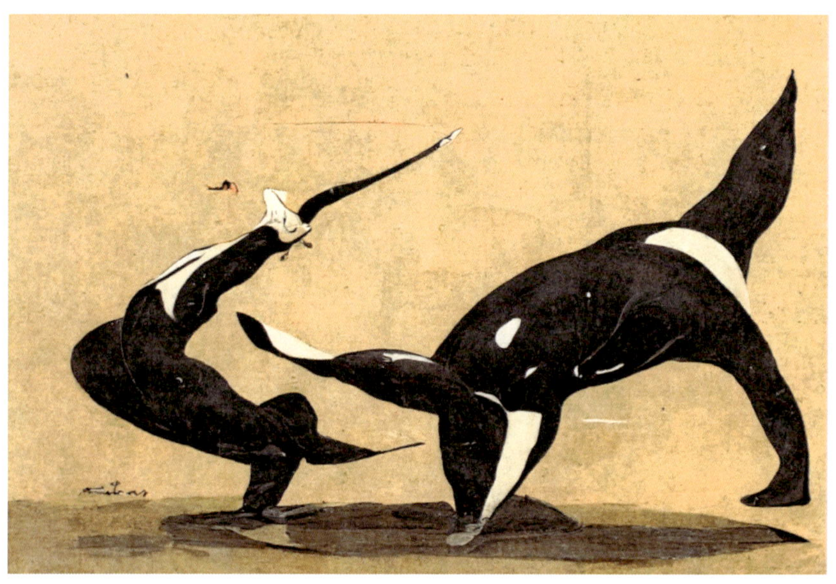

The eternal battle between acrobats and orcas.

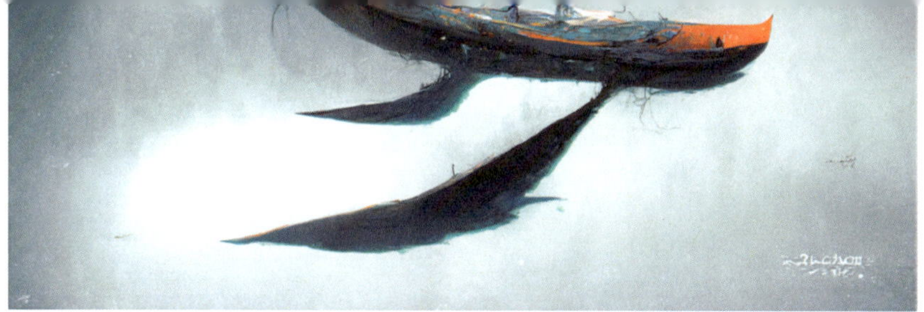

Midjourney AI often adds faux signatures to the images. The AI has learned that squiggly, signature-looking marks often go in the bottom right-hand corner of paintings.

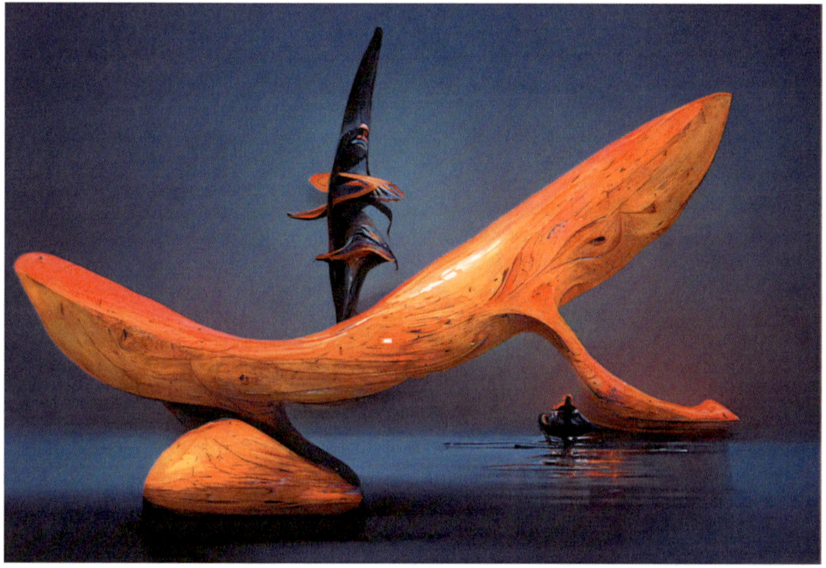

One big surprise in working with the AI was its ability to output illustrations that look like sculptures. I added "in the style of a wood sculpture" to the base prompt for this image.

EVA, CAN I SEE BEES IN A CAVE?

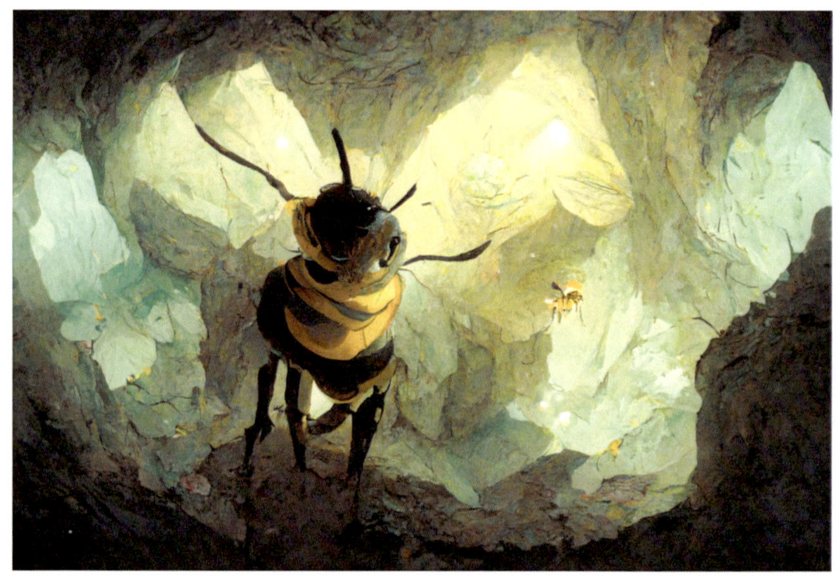

Cave bees!

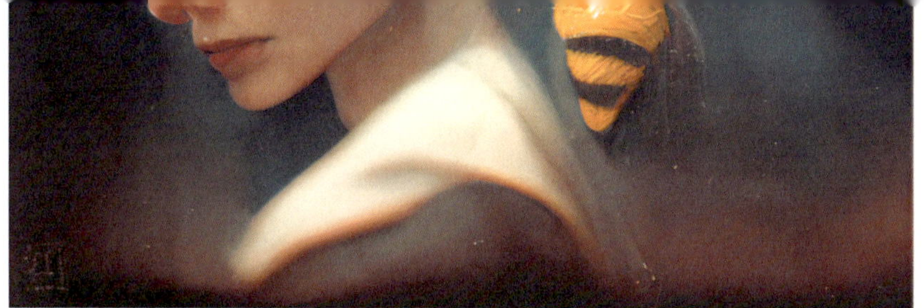

If she holds very still, maybe the huge cave bee will fly away.

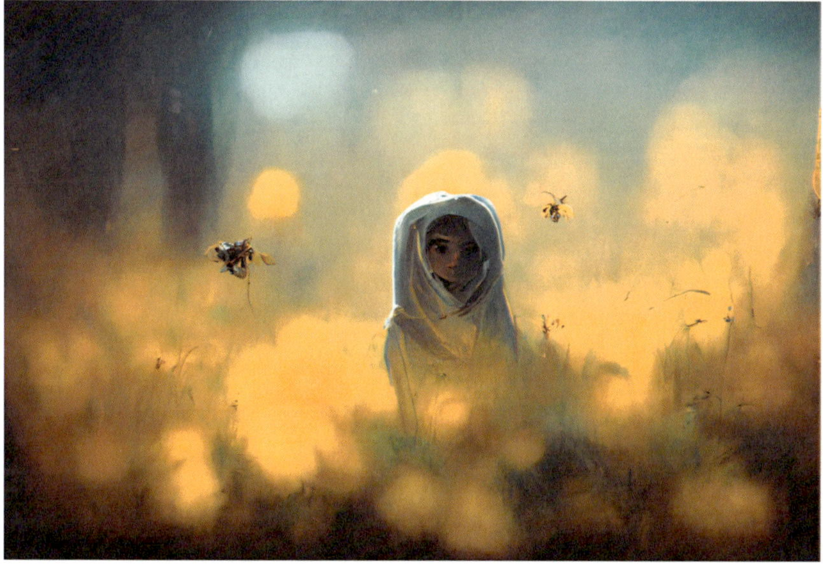

This must be Eva. The color of the flowers is inspired by the yellow that the AI associates with the color of bees.

BIRD RIB

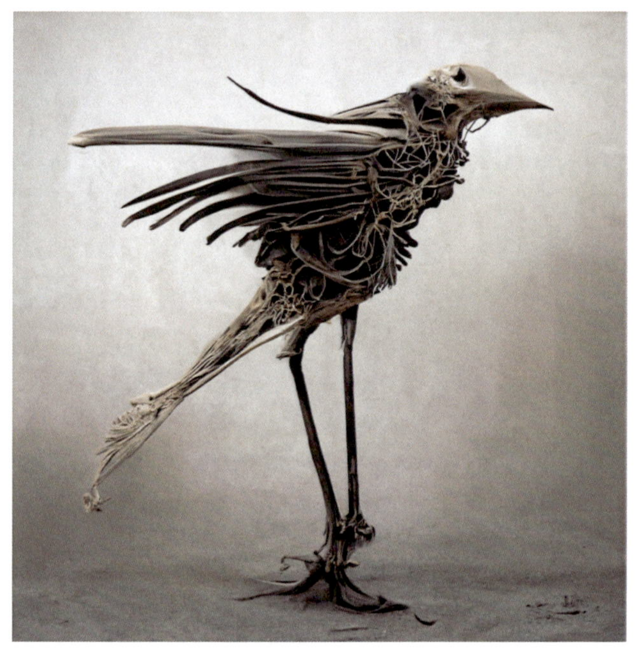

It took my breath away when this image rendered. I made a whole series of bone bird variations for my own collection.

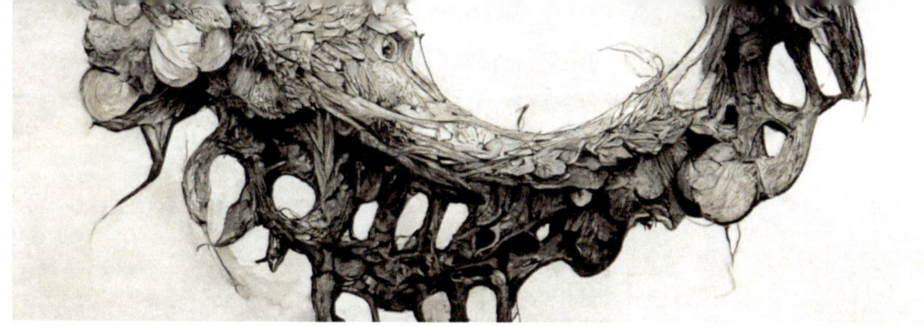

Here is a very different treatment. I add “detailed pencil drawing” or “detailed ink” to get images with this look.

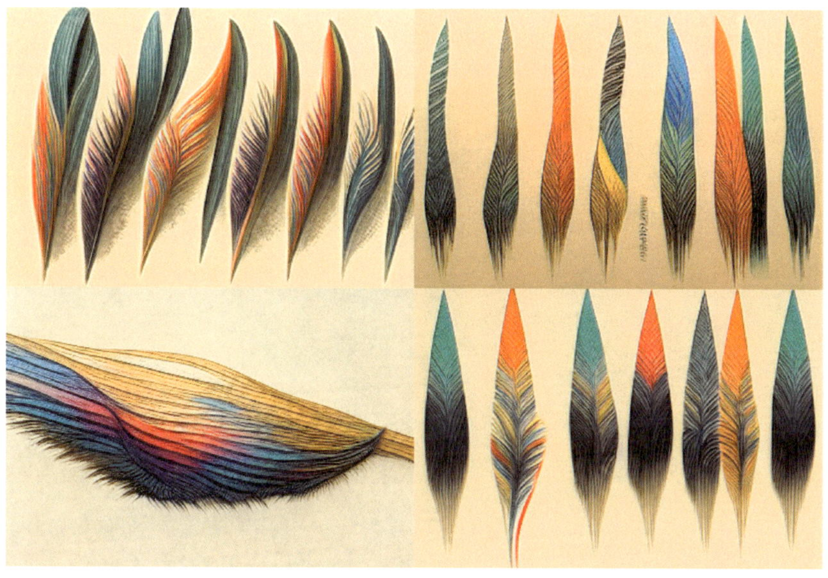

Bird feathers have ribs, too. This image is an example of the four thumbnail images the AI generates. You can pick the ones that hold promise to develop further.

CIGAR? TOSS IT IN A CAN. IT IS SO TRAGIC!

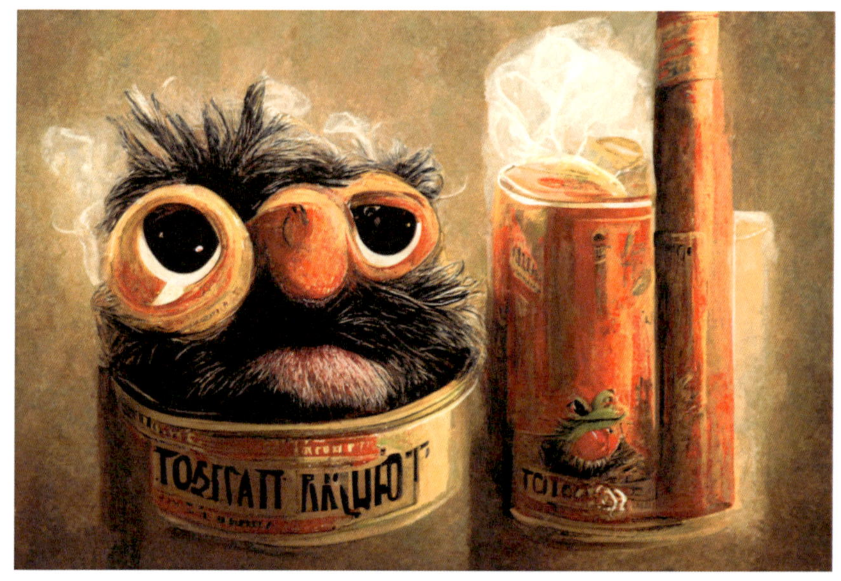

I added “in the style of muppets” to the palindrome prompt. The letters on the can come from the prompt. The AI associates smoke with the word cigar.

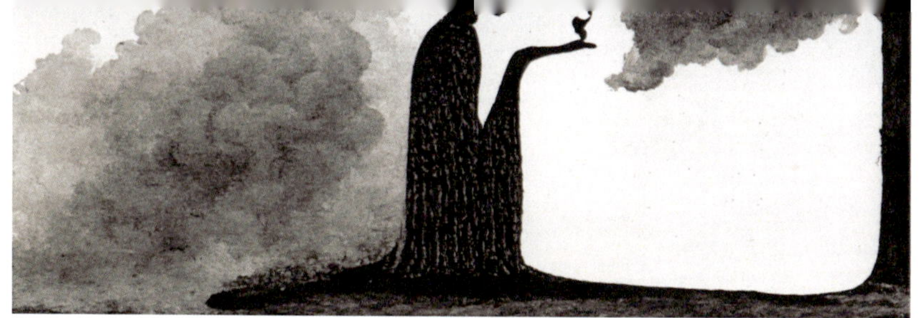

I added “in the style of Edward Gorey” to the palindrome prompt. Midjourney can mimic the style of many famous artists and art schools.

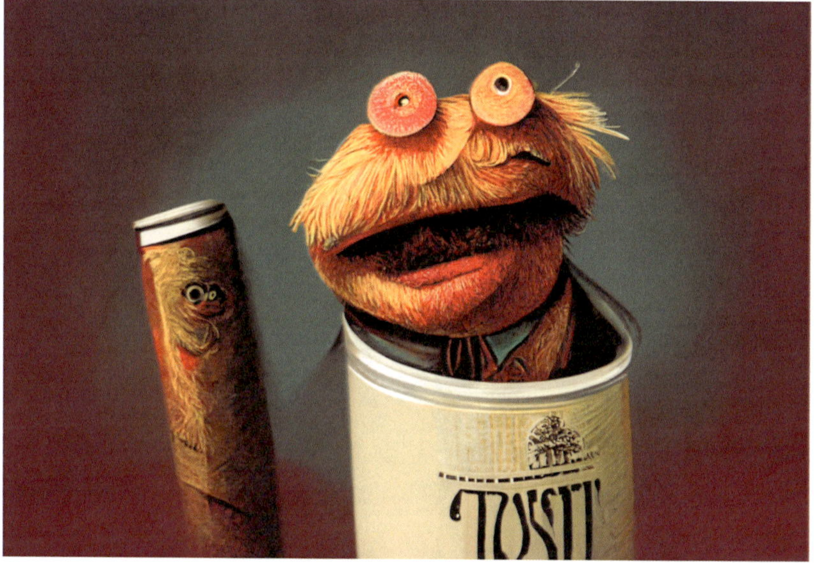

Another muppet in a can. My sense of humor is so tragic.

DID I DRAW DELLA TOO TALL, EDWARD? I DID!

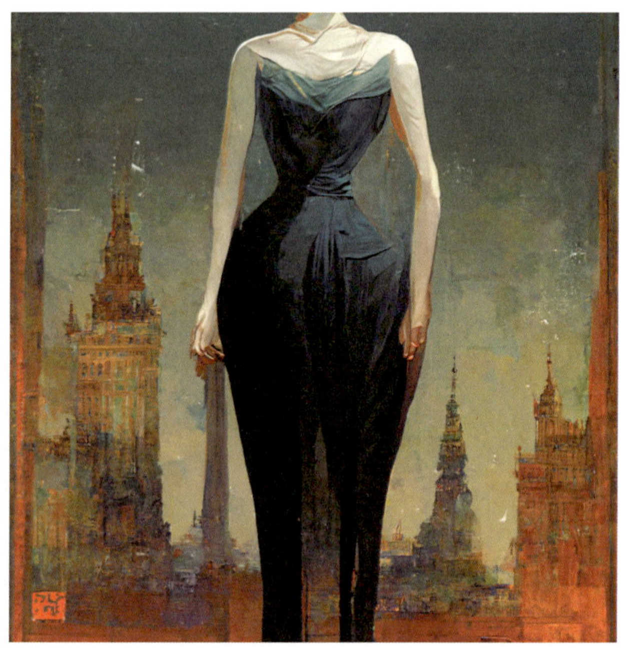

Art-directing an AI. I specified "very tall woman" and a square image format to get Midjourney to draw the woman with her head out of the image.

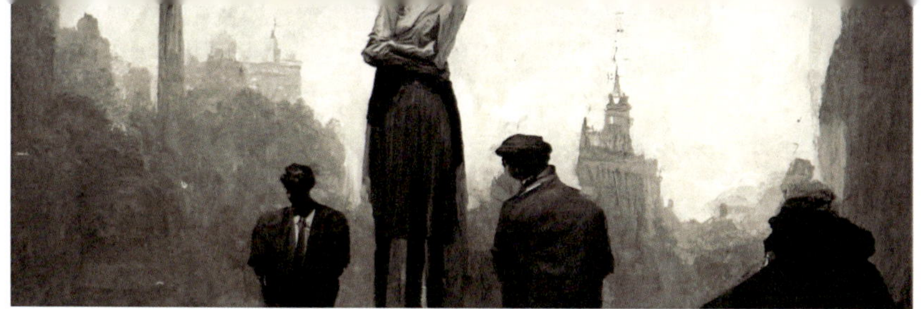

Here is another example of the AI drawing in the style of an artist. I added “in style of artist George Bellows.” MidJourney got it, even drawing the image in black and white and dressing the people in early 20th century clothes.

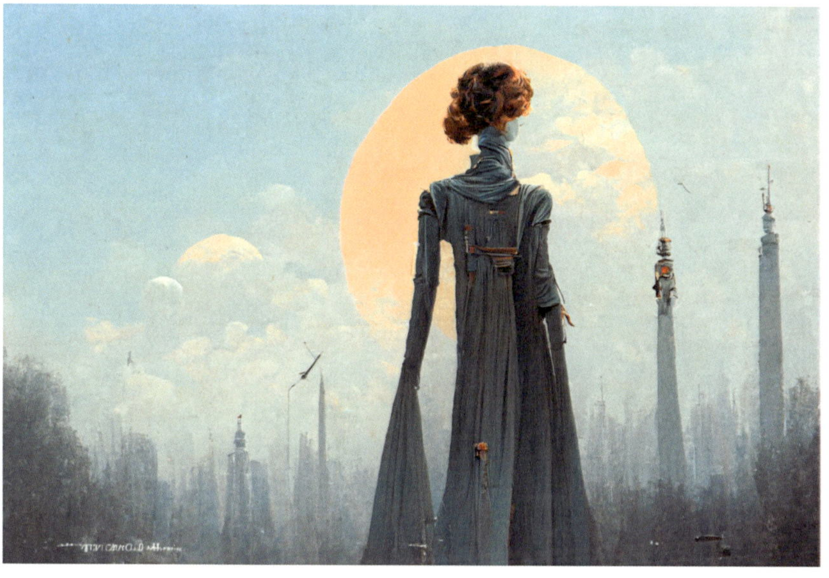

Here I added “in the style of Star Wars” for this very tall woman. The force was with me.

DO GEESE SEE GOD?

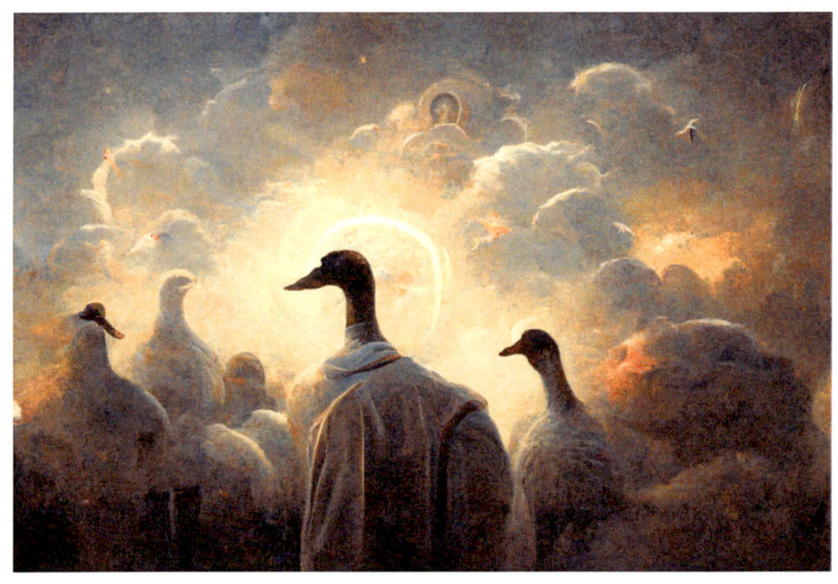

Magic AI eight-ball says, “Yes, definitely. Geese do see God.”

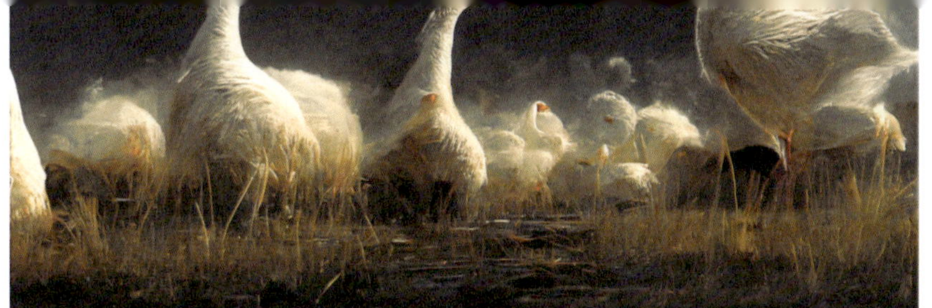

Magic AI eight-ball says, "No. The geese were looking in the wrong direction."

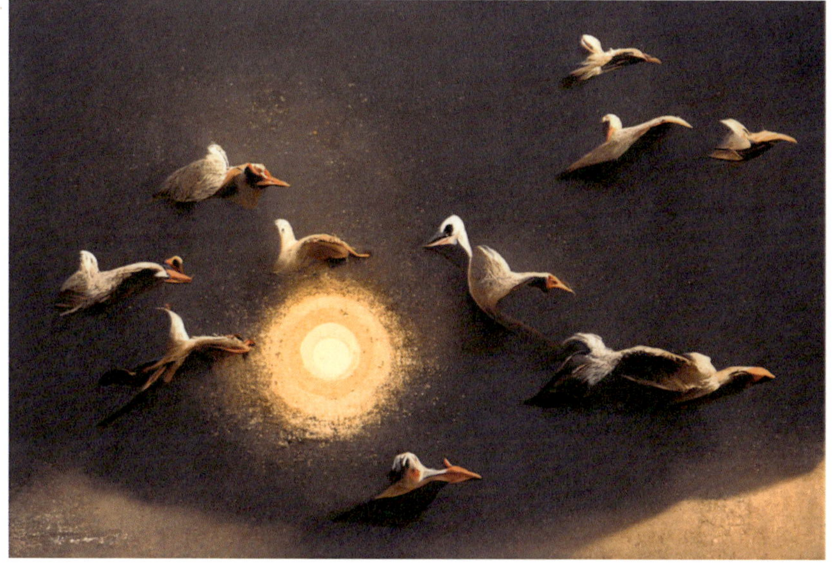

What a time to be alive!

DOC NOTE, I DISSENT, A FAST NEVER PREVENTS A FATNESS. I DIET ON COD

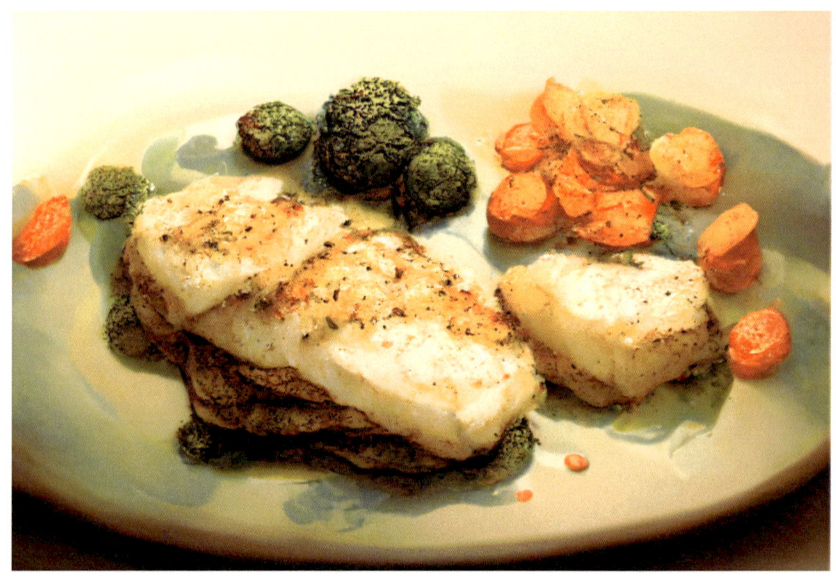

MidJourney is surprisingly good at drawing cod fillets. Those carrots look tasty, too.

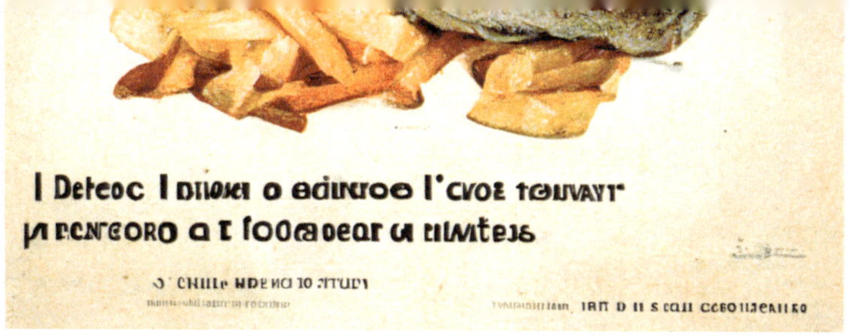

The AI also apparently knows how to draw can labels for frog-thing with french fries. Love the handy fork tail and the encouraging "Do = Doc!"

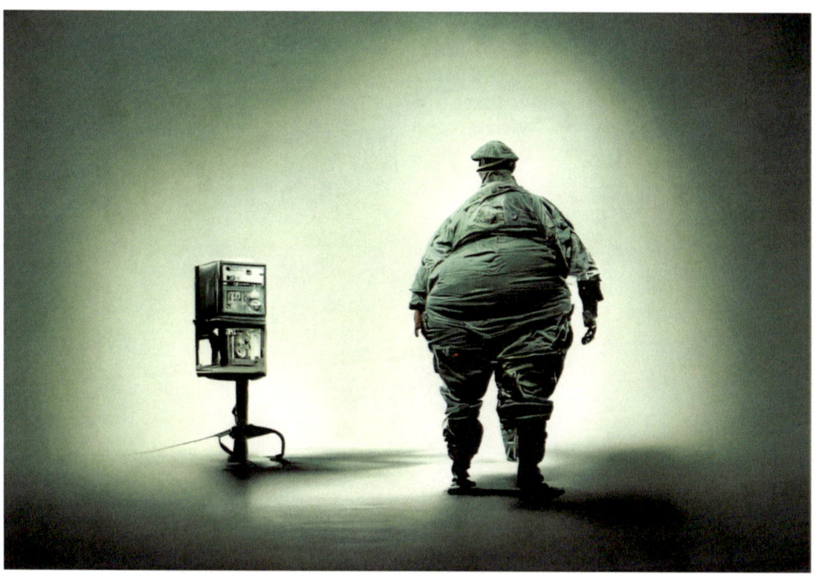

For this try the AI focused on the words Doc and Fatness in the prompt. Notice how it lighted the image and added shadows. The AI system has learned a lot about art technique from the half-billion images it was trained on.

DOG, AS A DEVIL DEIFIED, LIVED AS A GOD

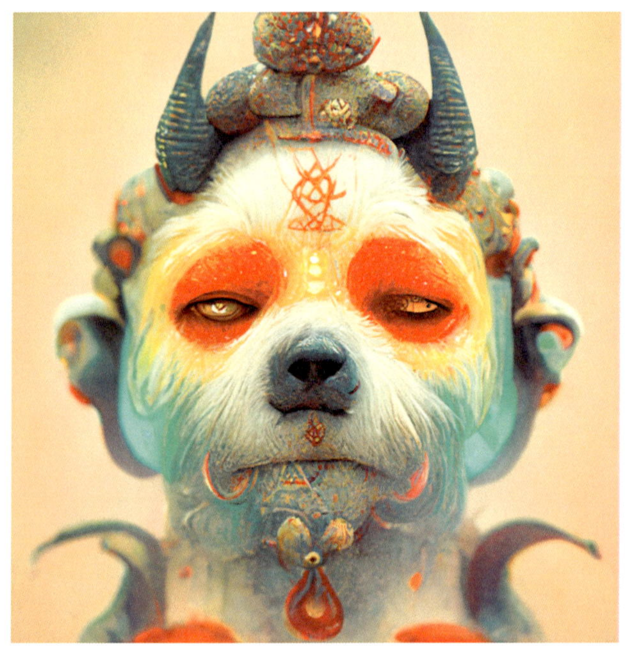

I was getting a lot of red devil dogs, so I added "Hindu deity" for a whole different dog vibe.

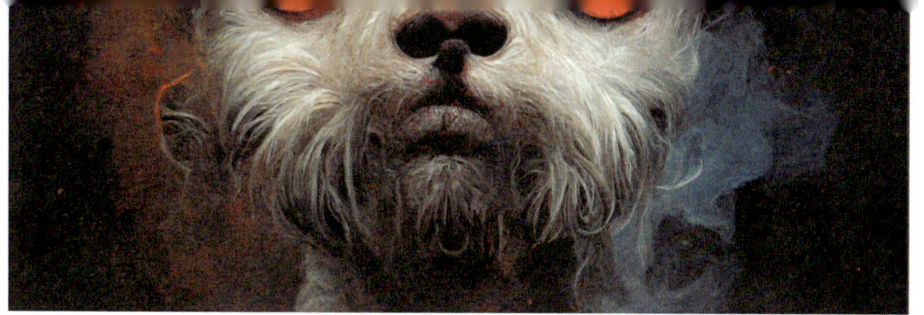

Classic devil dog perfection.

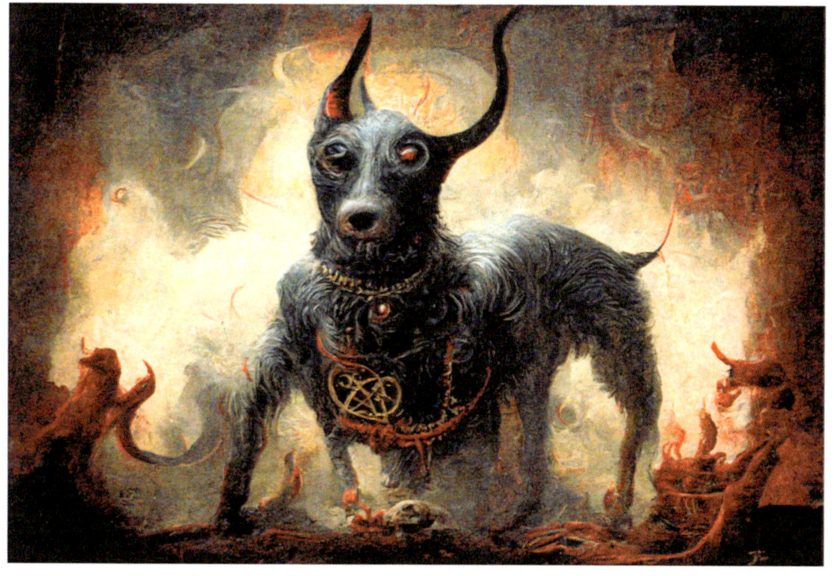

This is literally my neighbor's dog.

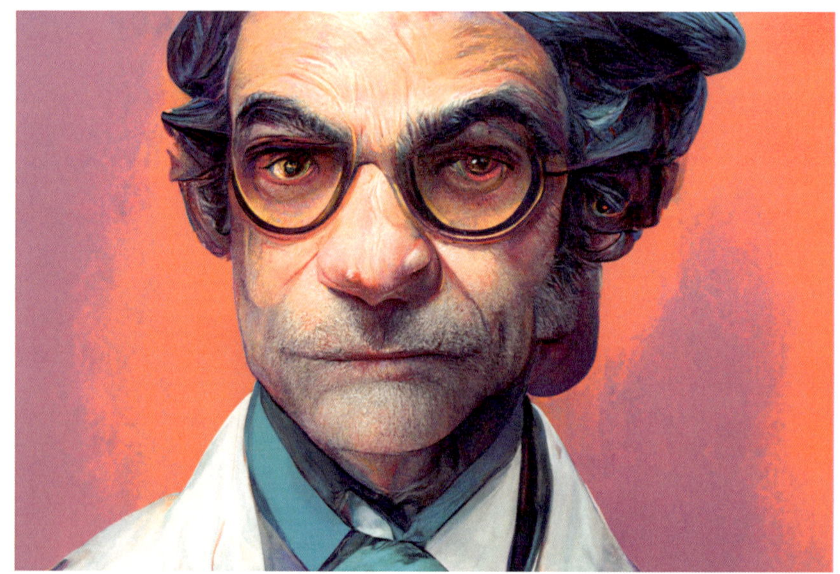

Say Ahhhh.

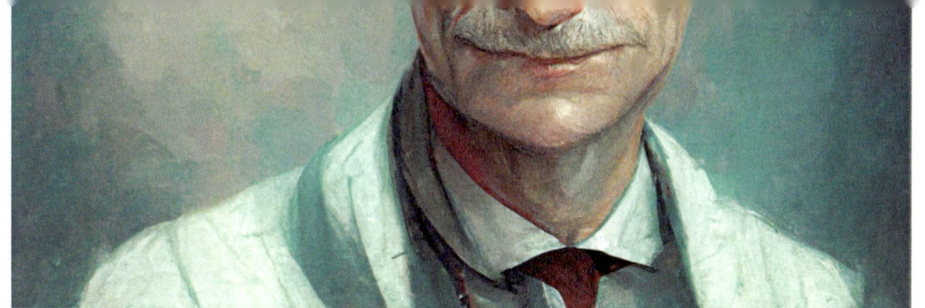

Maybe not awkward. Maybe just tired. Notice that the AI strongly associates white coats with the word doctor in all these images.

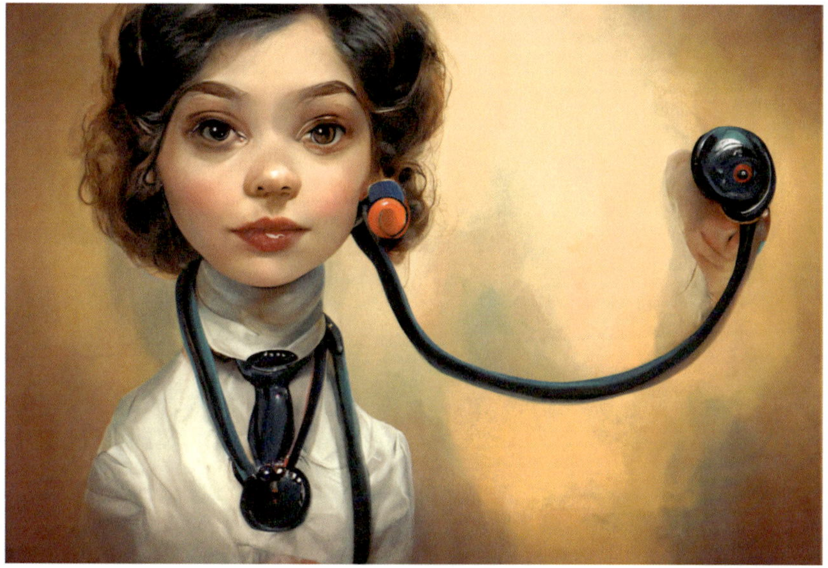

I added “stethoscope” to the prompt. Midjourney drew it: awkwardly. It knows stethoscopes go around the neck and in the ear, but it’s not sure exactly how to connect things up.

DRAW, O COWARD

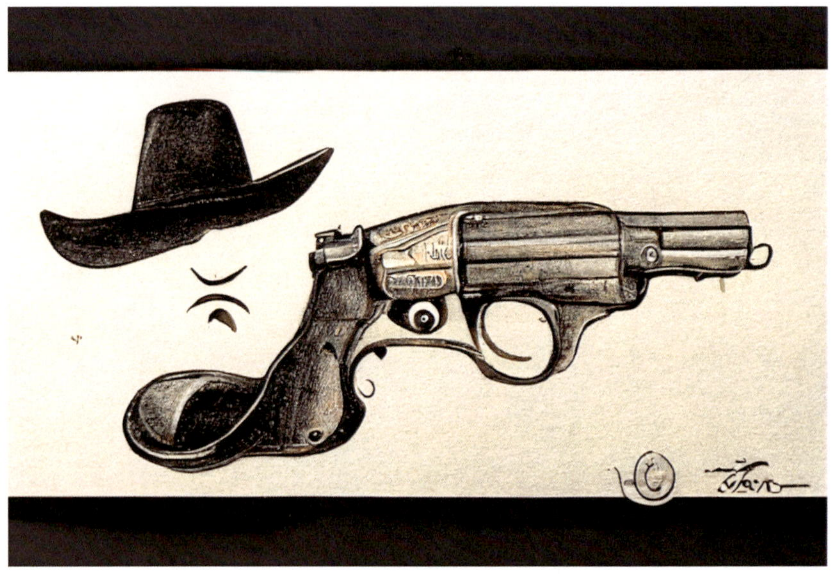

I added "cowboy" and "cartoon" to the prompt for this palindrome. Midjourney developed the unique pistol after a long series of variations.

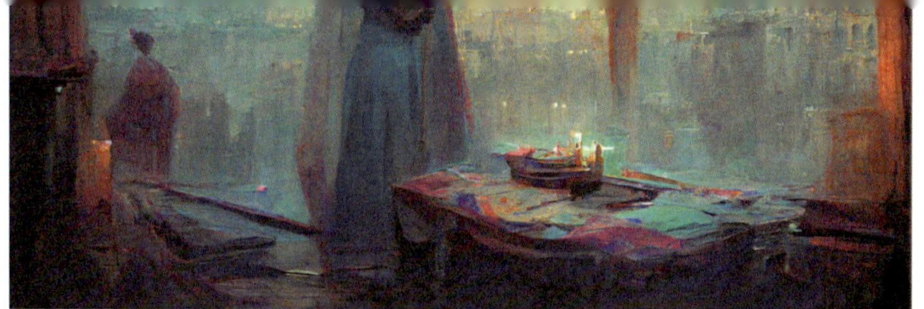

MidJourney is no coward about drawing, but it does think placing figures looking away from the viewer is super cool.

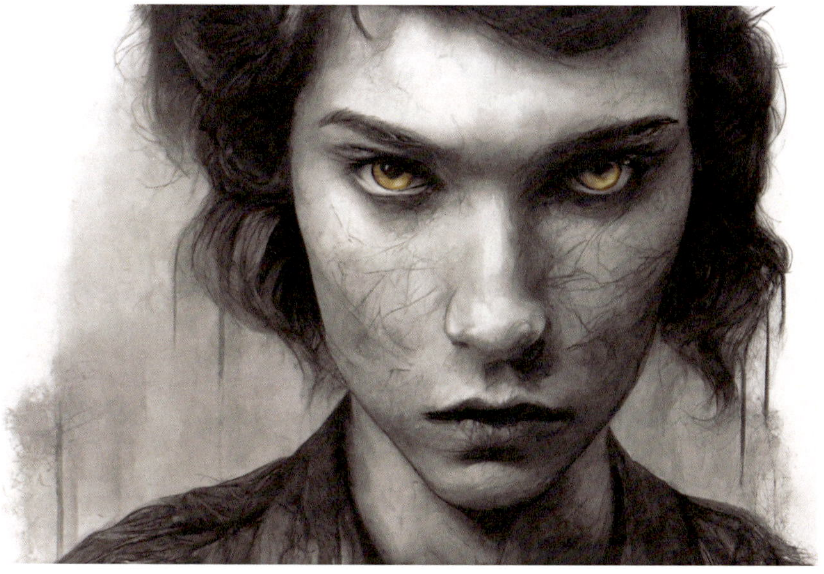

Made with a test version of Midjourney that was much better with human eyes and noses. Apparently it was also very capable of drawing naughty pictures and doing realistic celebrity portraits. As with any powerful new technology, there will be accompanying legal and ethical questions.

DRAWER AS A REWARD

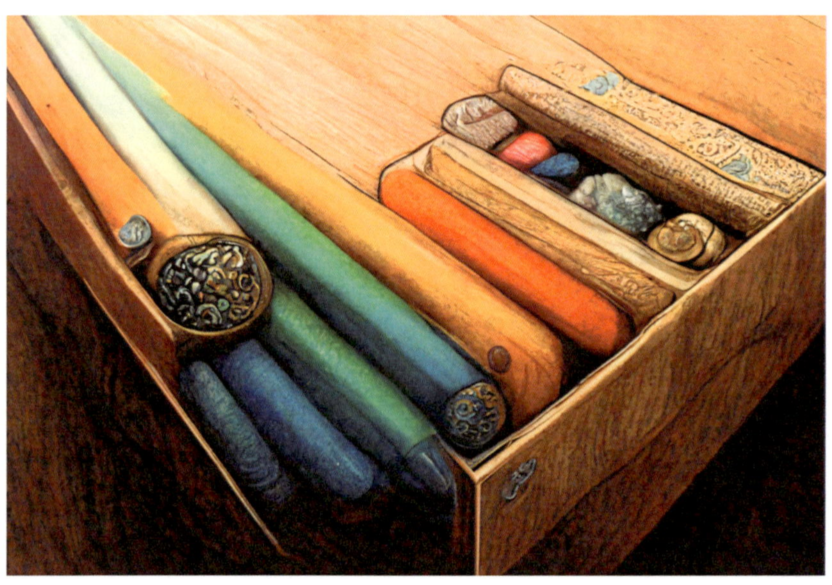

This series was a complete surprise. Definitely a reward for all my hard work in the pixel mines.

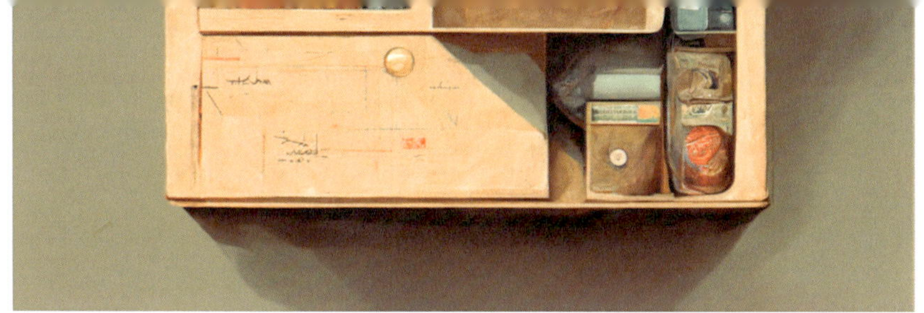

Where did this even come from? I added "shop-drawing" to the prompt.

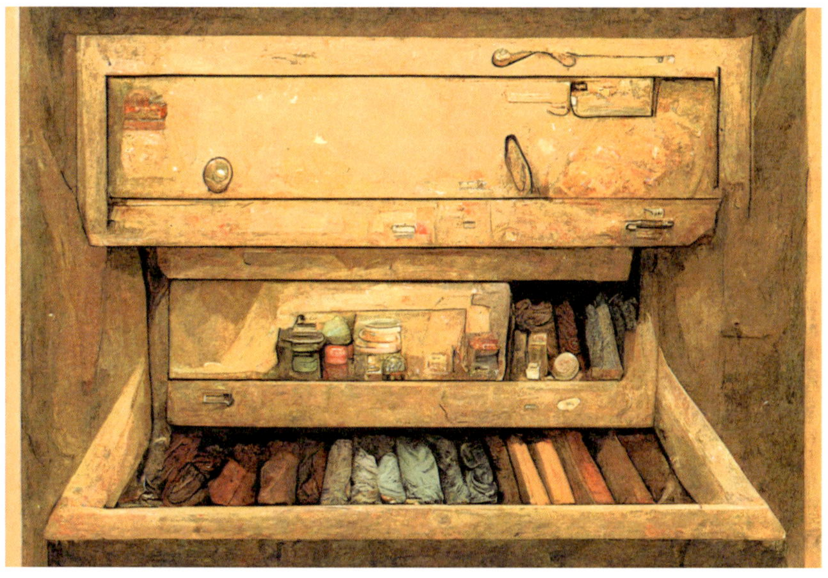

Another drawer as a reward. I added "colored pencil" to the prompt.

EVIL OLIVE

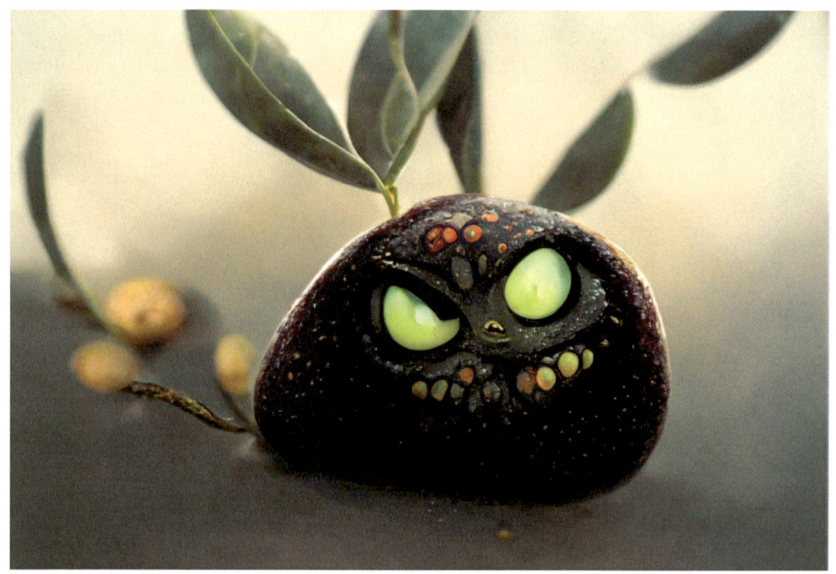

Who ever thought that evil could be this cute.

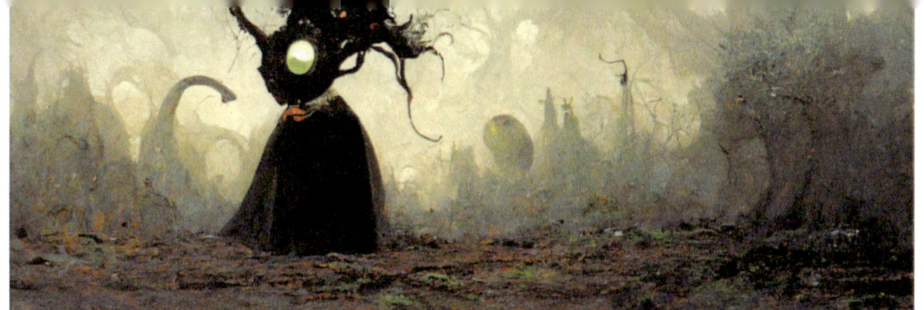

Another kind of evil olive.

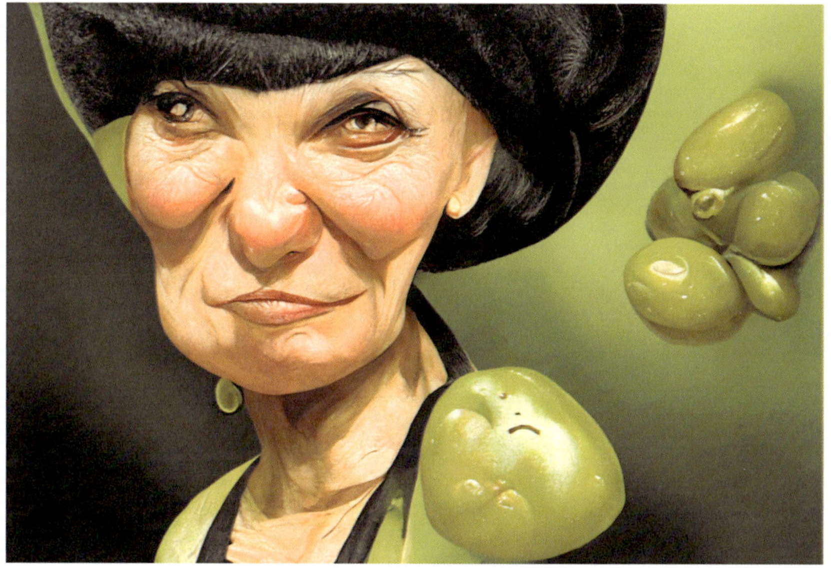

Ms. Olive E. Ville. Notice how Midjourney picked olive colors for her clothes.

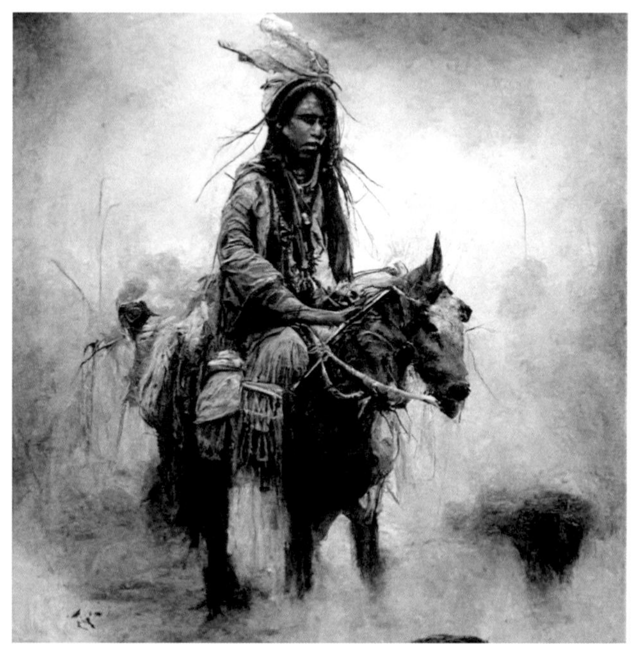

One of my favorite images. It was very difficult to get a person riding a horse. Luck and persistence pays off in the pixel mines.

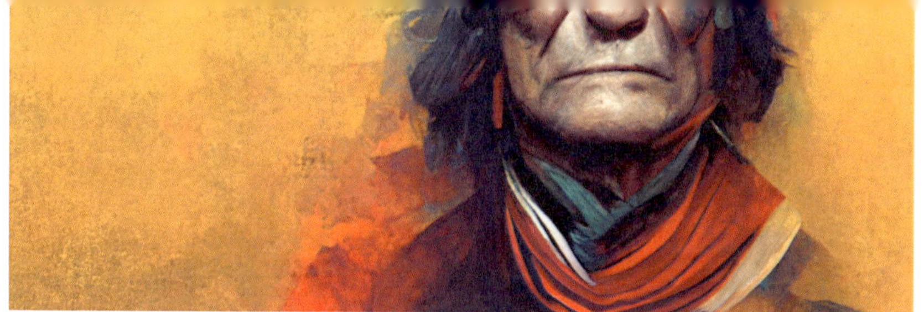

This is a good example of using a name in the prompt to get the figure facing forward. The actual historical figure had more of a shorter, rounder face.

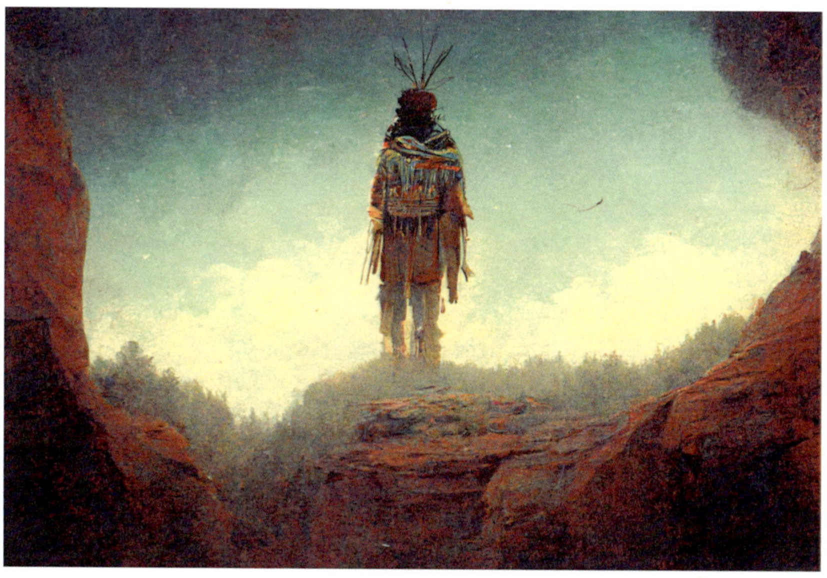

It is interesting to see what type of visual associations the AI draws from Geronimo, a Native American from the 1800s. How does it influence the AI's color choice? The setting and landscape? The character's dress and features?

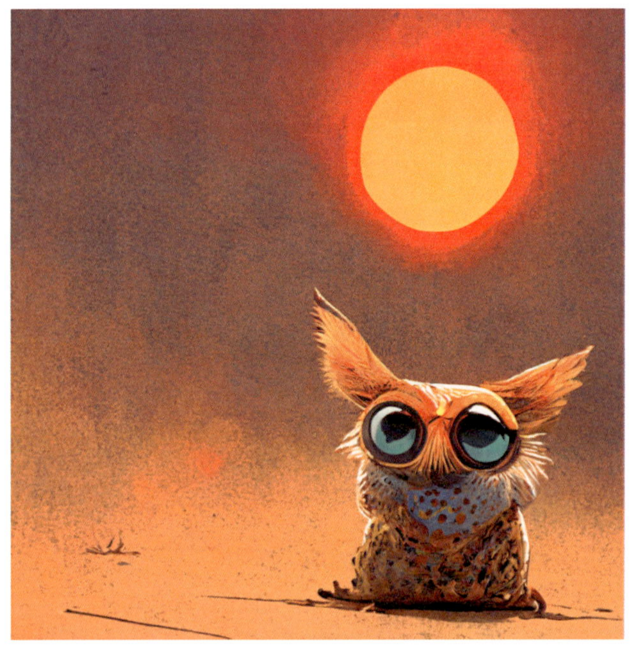

So cute!

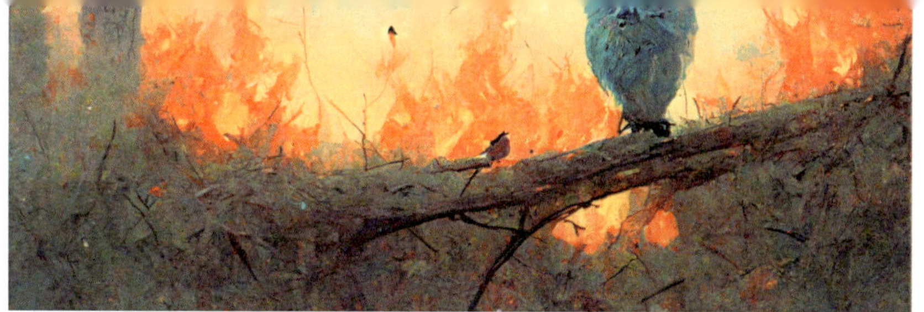

Mr. Owl is saving his hoots for another day.

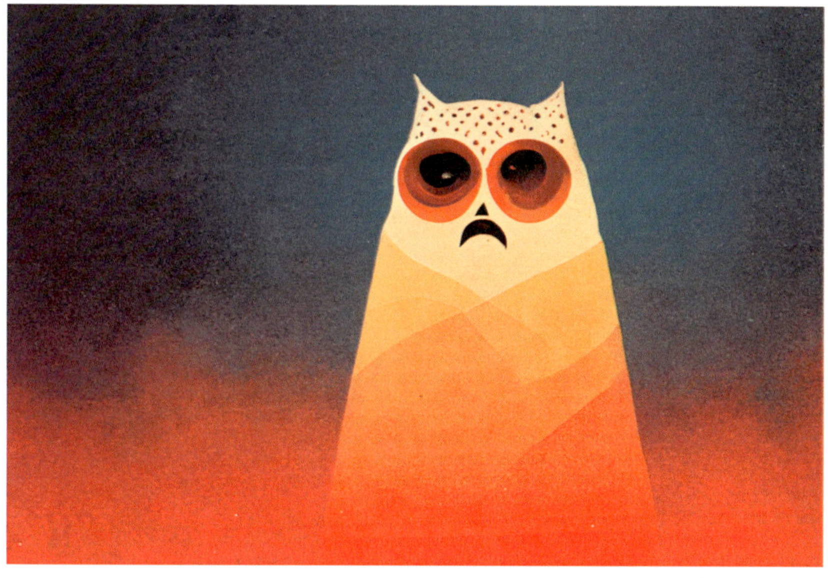

Added “in the style of a poster” to the prompt for this one.

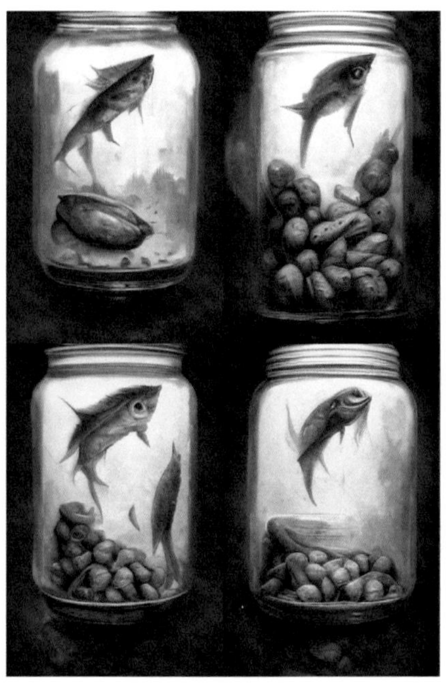

Here is an example of the four small images first generated from the palindrome prompt. Which one would you pick to develop?

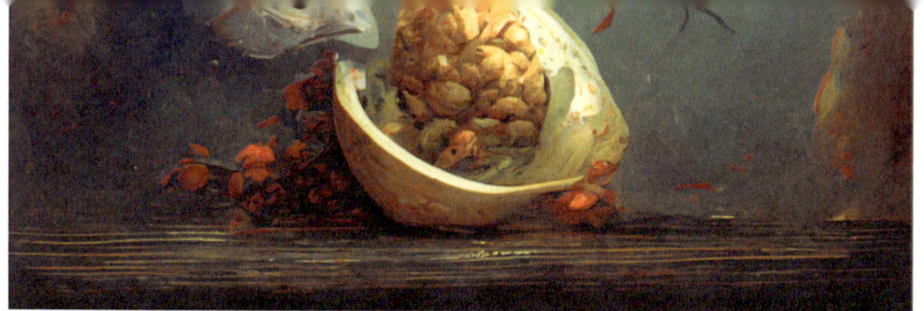

How about a tuna tasting a walnut underwater? No jar in this illustration. Maybe the whole scene is in a jar.

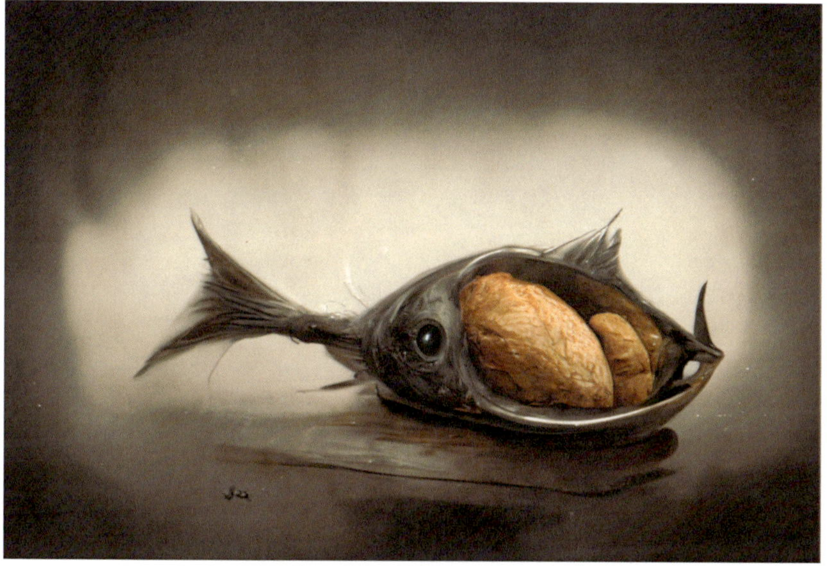

A fish as a dish! People are already using the image generation capability to inspire real-world products: I know of cakes, shoes, games, dolls and purses so far.

AMY, MUST I JUJITSU MY MA?

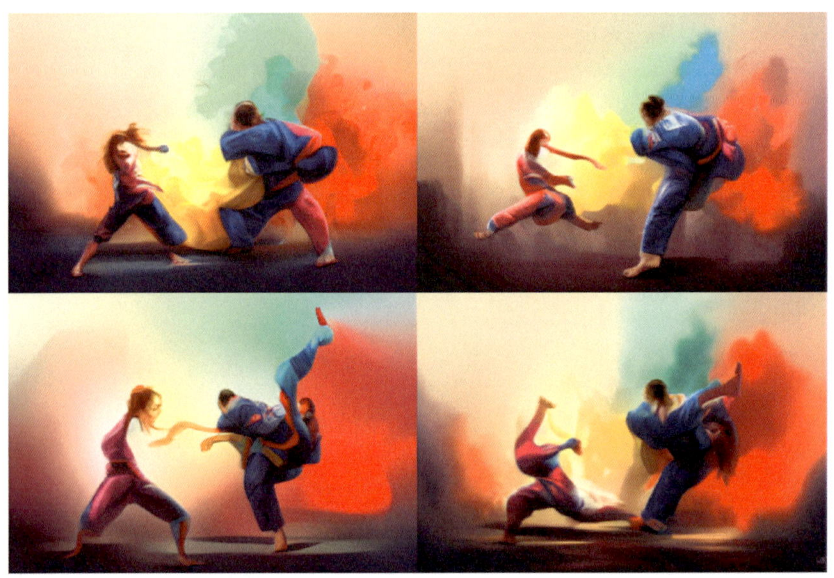

This shows the original images generated by the palindrome prompt. Distorted figures like this are really common, especially with a prompt word like jujitsu. The colors are great, though.

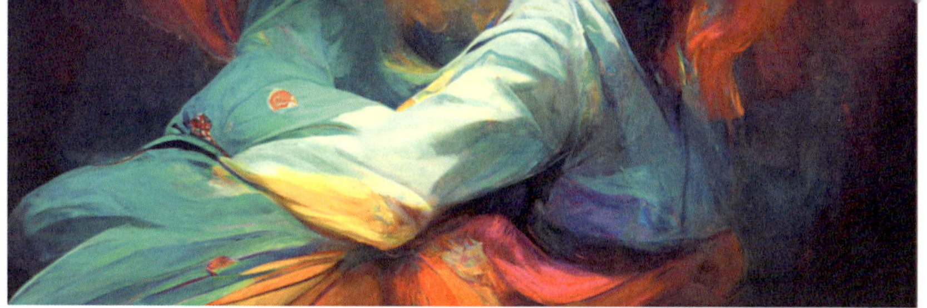

I could never get the bodies or face perfect, but the feel and energy is all there. Anyone who has had a middle-school daughter knows this picture speaks the non-literal truth.

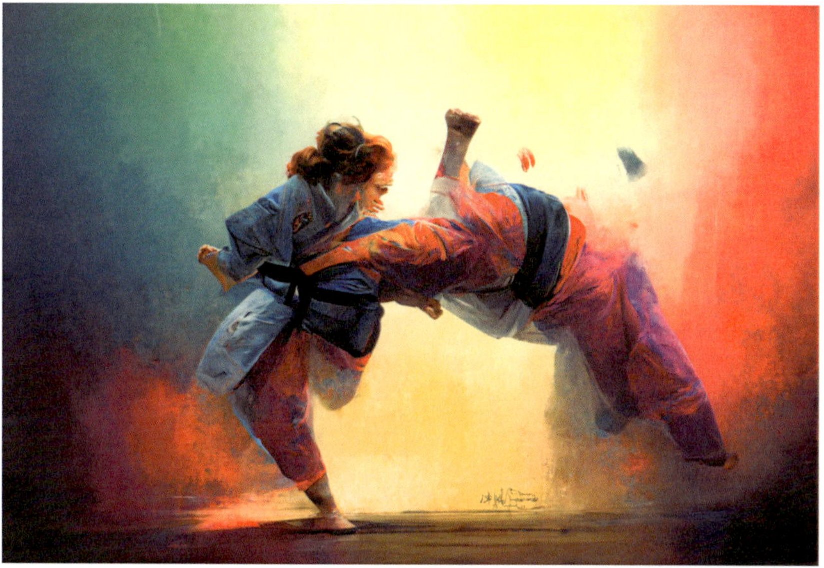

I love these colors and the dynamic pose. It is still hard to get two people or things to interact with Midjourney. It took a lot of failed attempts to get this.

KAYAK SALAD, ALASKA YAK

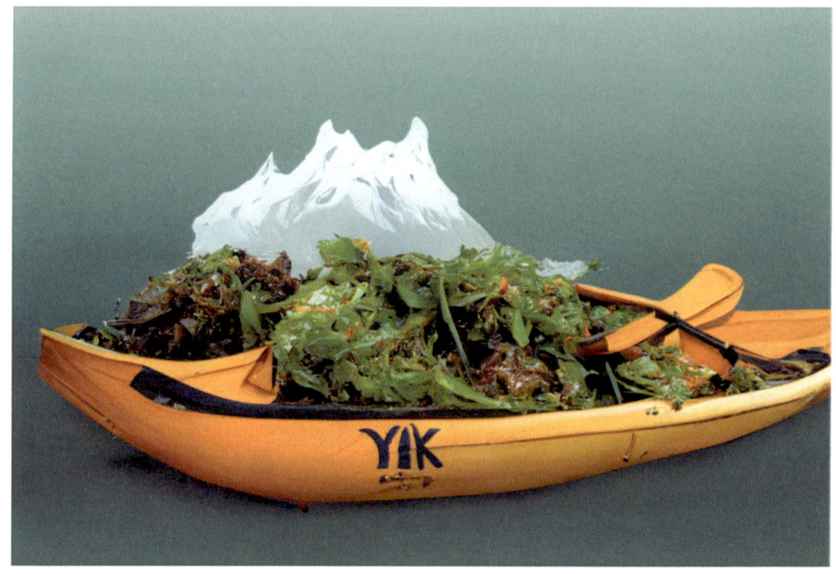

Salad in a kayak. Alaska mountains implied in the background. Once again, Midjourney AI sneaks in a word from the prompt: the kayak is named Yak.

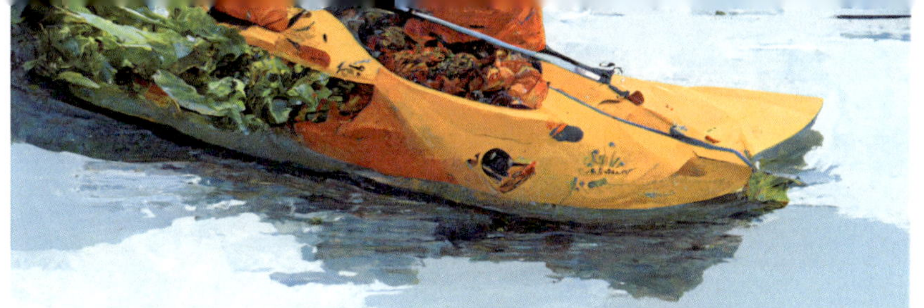

I'm sure that ice-cold Alaskan water will keep the kayaker's salad fresh

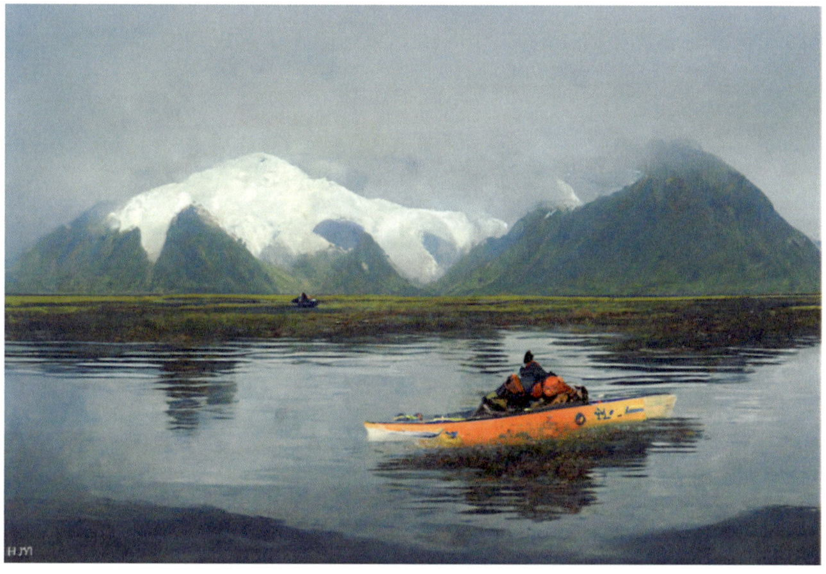

What does Midjourney associate with the prompt words Alaska and Kayak? Snow-covered mountains rising close to the sea, reflections in the water, mist partially obscuring the mountain tops, the bright color of a kayak. None of that was specified directly in the prompt. Amazing!

LIVE NOT ON EVIL

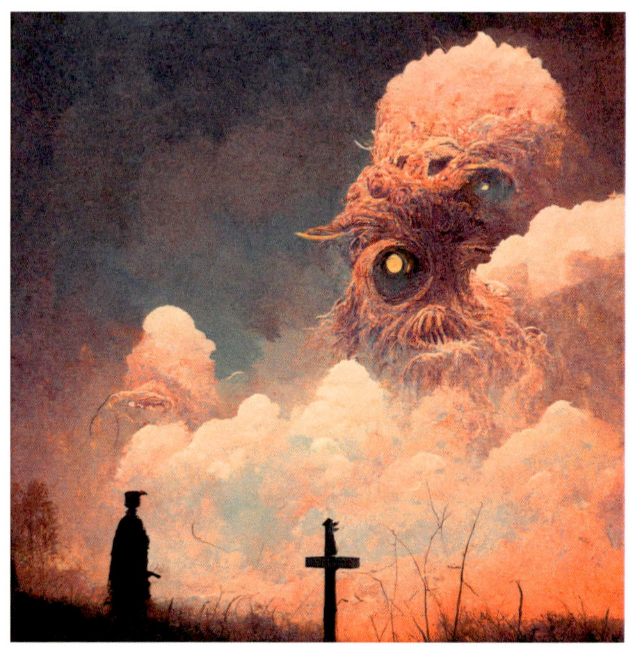

“Live not on Evil.” Great advice. Midjourney captured it perfectly in this moody piece complete with ominous cloud monster.

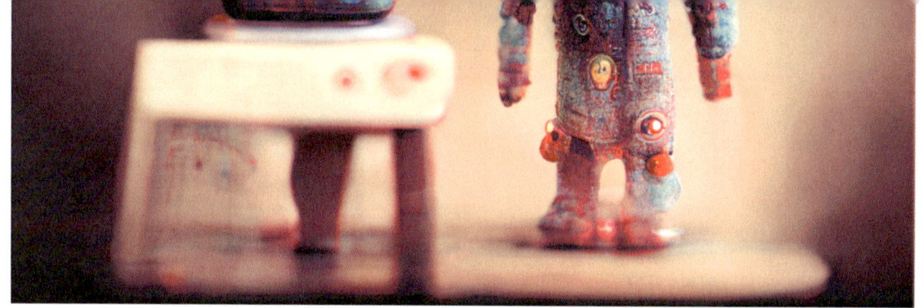

Same prompt with the addition of "toy." Midjourney supplies an evil toy, evil toy colors, evil brown background, and hilariously misspelled prompt words on the TV. The evil toy is probably also a choking hazard.

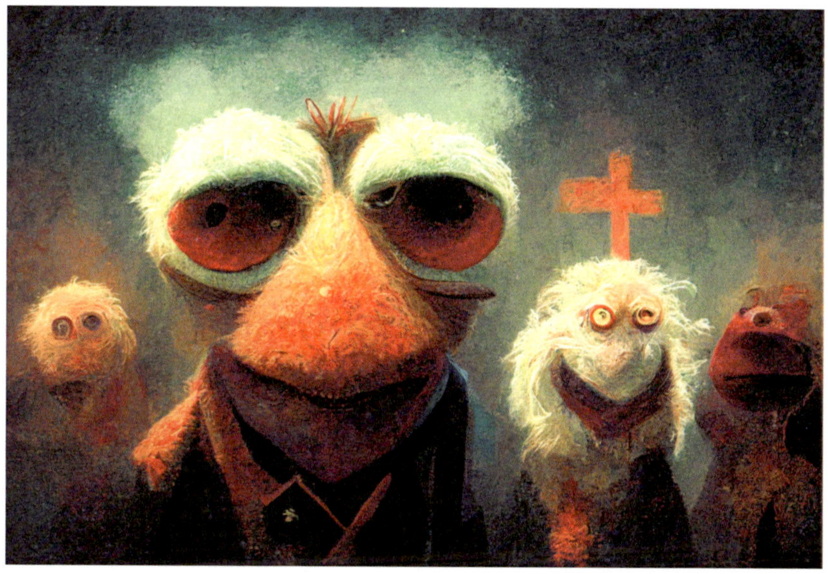

Live not on evil. A final warning—Muppet style!

LOL

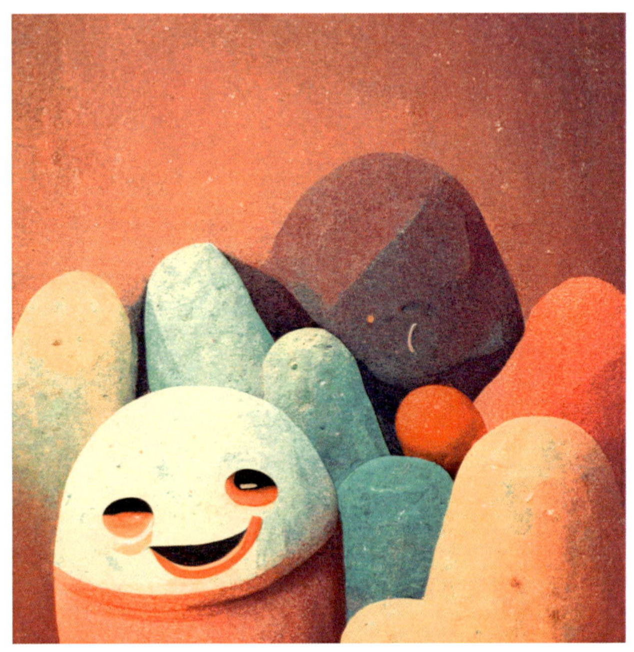

LOL stands for "Laugh out Loud." I was curious how Midjourney would respond to the prompt. This output made me LOL.

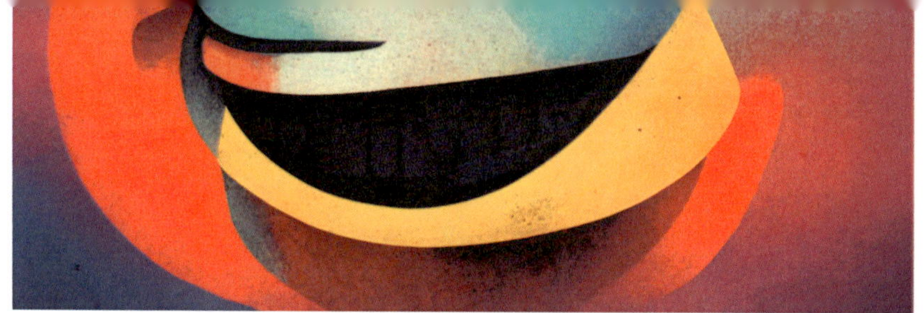

I tried the LOL prompt many times. Over and over, Midjourney output variations of a big happy-face using specific colors. It's the LOL emoji!

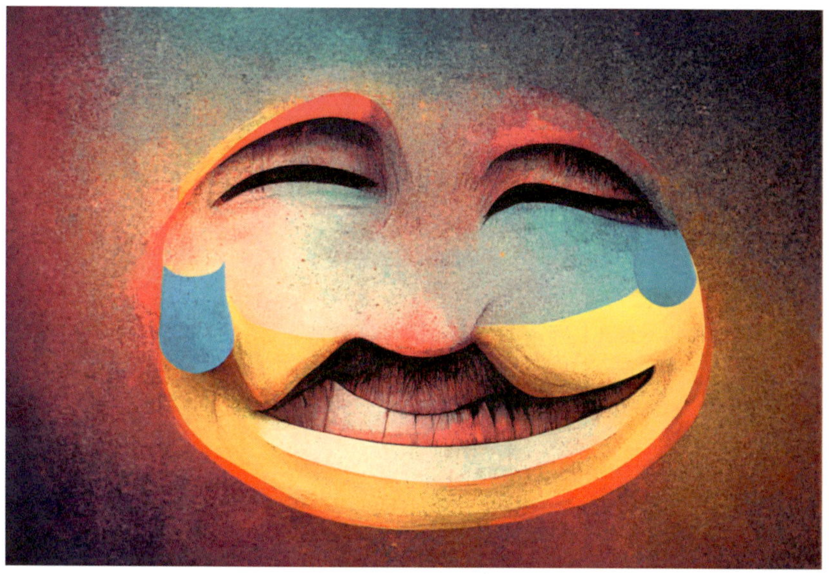

Here are the blue tears of laughter common on a popular LOL emoji. Midjourney also started drawing a human face behind the emoji. How metaphoric!

MADAM, I'M ADAM

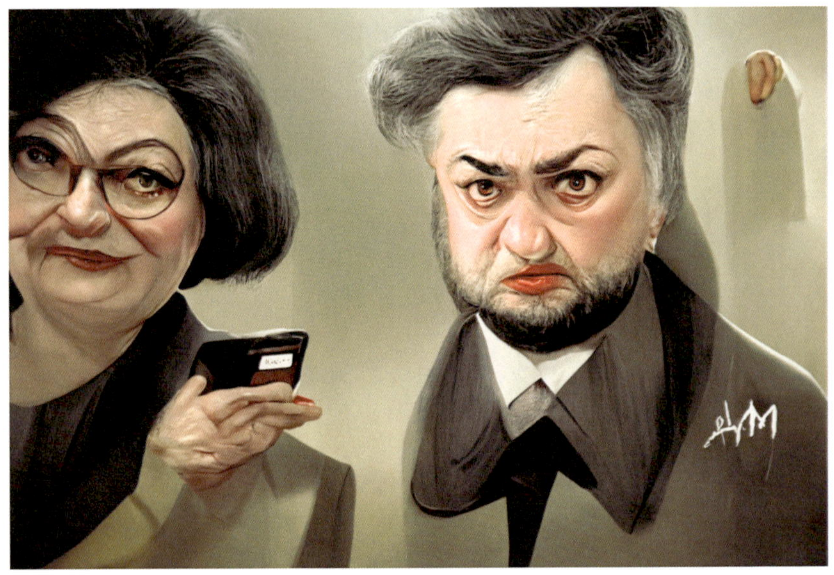

Midjourney's cartoon rendering of a palindrome classic. What expressions!

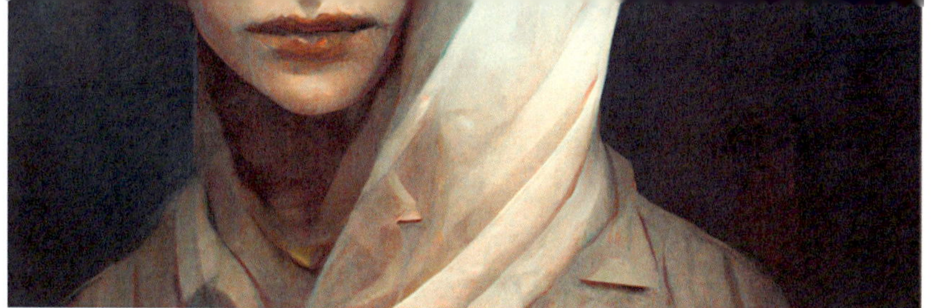

Adam I'm Madam? Or maybe Adam as Madam. A nice androgynous portrait with beautiful painterly lighting.

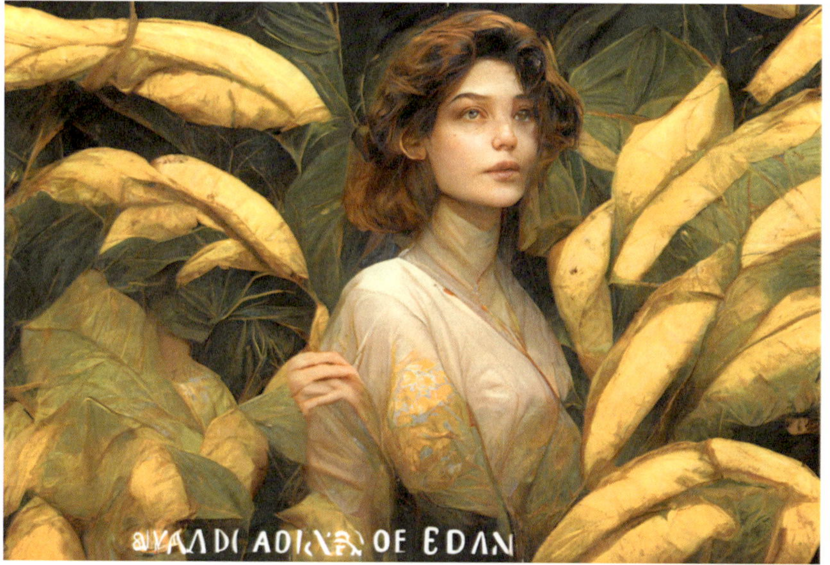

I added "in the garden of Eden" to the prompt to see if I could get Adam and Eve wearing fig leaves. Midjourney has been trained not to produce nudes to avoid becoming a font of unlimited naughty. Should restrictions like this be placed on AI image generation? If so, where should lines be drawn?

MAY A MOODY BABY DOOM A YAM

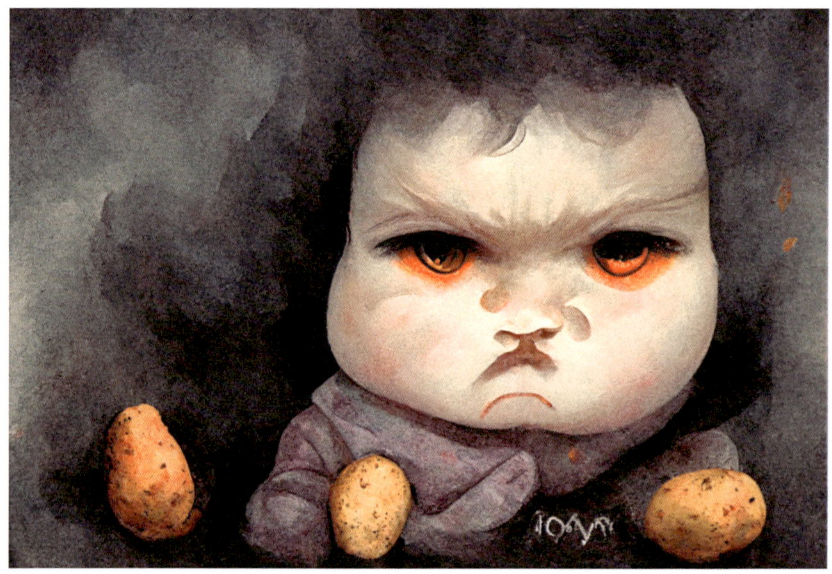

Such a moody baby, but those yams look a lot like Yukon Gold potatoes. Working with the AI, you take what you can get. No way currently to keep this moody baby while also specifying more yammy yams.

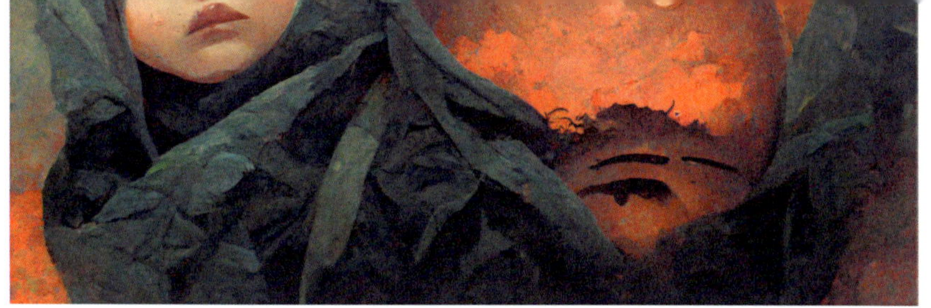

I asked for a moody baby dooming a yam in the style of the legendary Japanese animation studio, Studio Ghibli. Here is a moody baby and the yam doomed to save her.

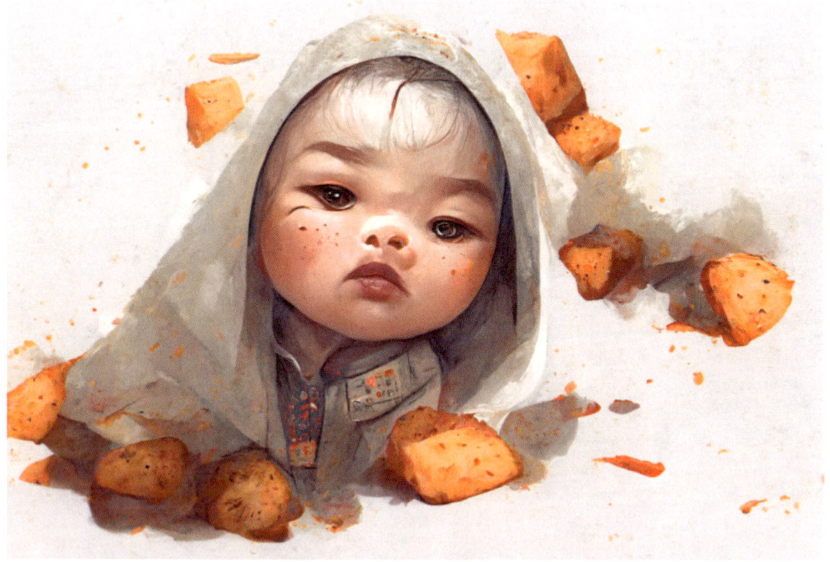

I asked for a Chinese baby dooming a yam. Midjourney thought the yams should be stir-fried, seasoned, and served with soy-sauce-colored shading.

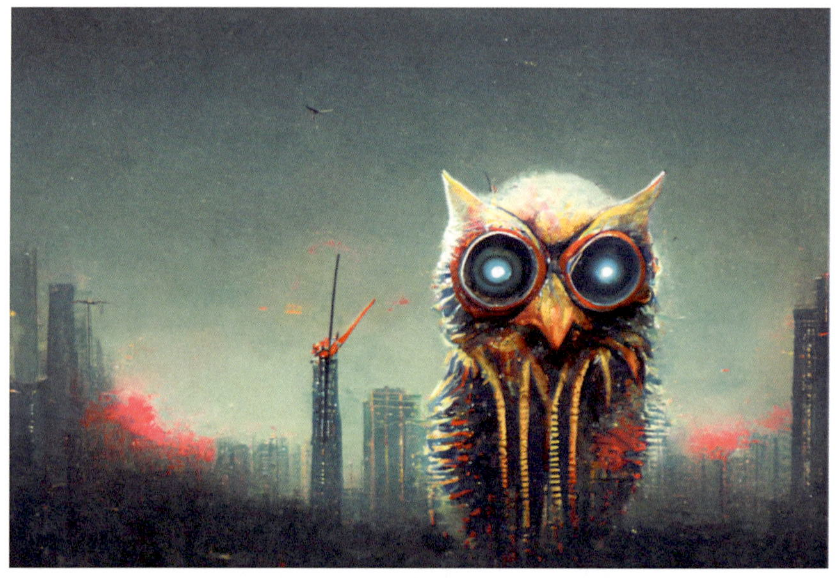

A cyberpunk owl in a post-apocalyptic landscape. He looks like he could easily digest a metal worm.

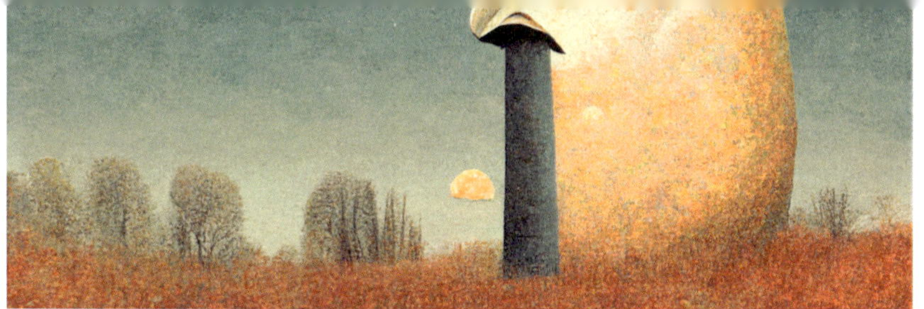

A surreal Mr. Owl, caught mid-meal

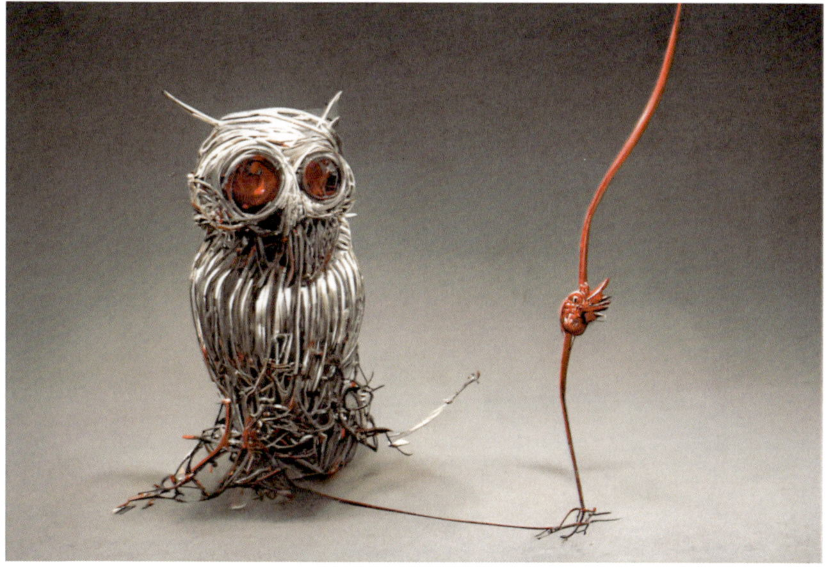

Added “in the style of a silver wire sculpture” to the base prompt. Midjourney is very capable of producing photographic-looking illustrations.

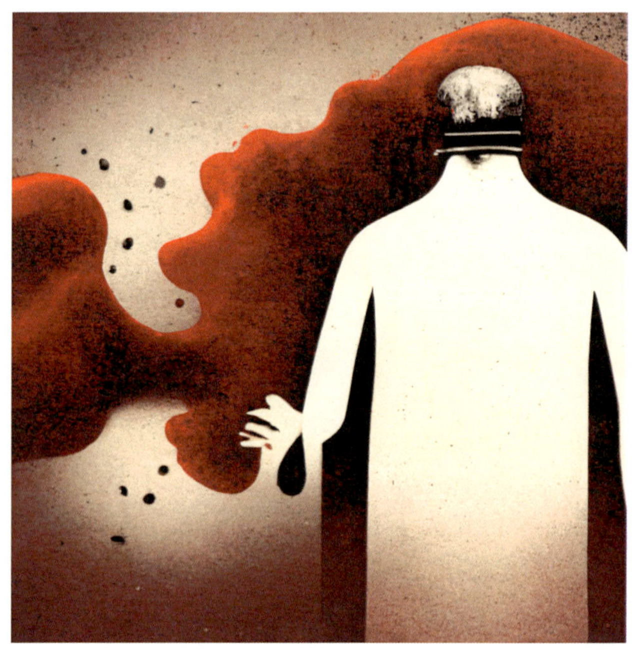

A great book cover for a murder mystery.
Authors are already using AI images for cover art
—including the cover of this book.

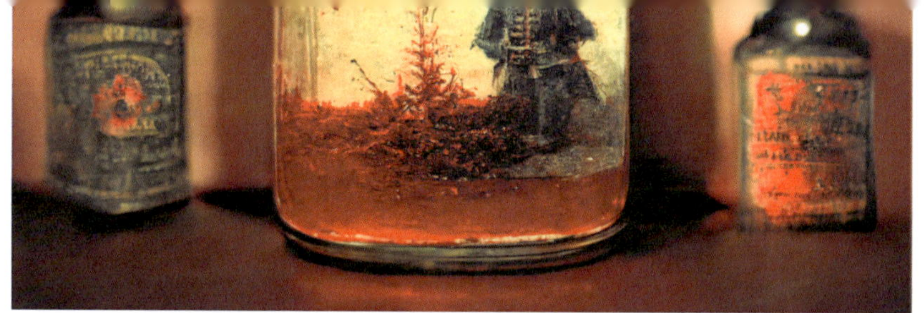

The AI associates murder with the color red. Even the labels on the bottles contain red.

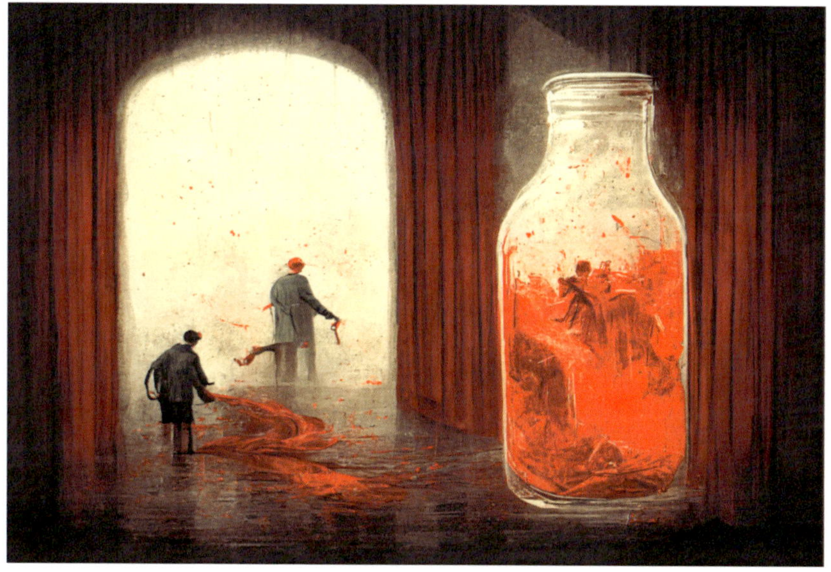

More murder, more red. Who are those mysterious figures fleeing the scene?

SOME MEN INTERPRET NINE MEMOS

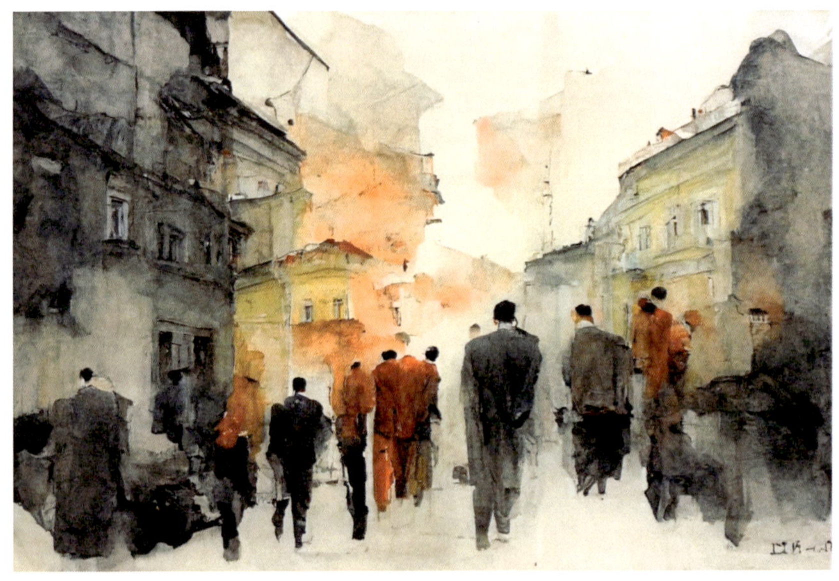

In this outdoor scene. Midjourney focuses on the men, not the memos.

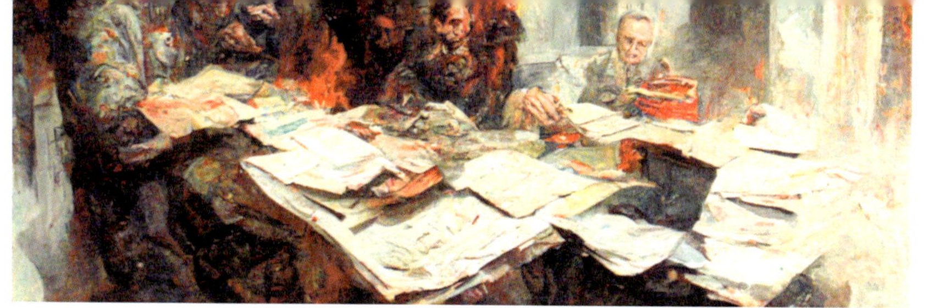

In this version, the memos are front and center. I hope none of them are classified.

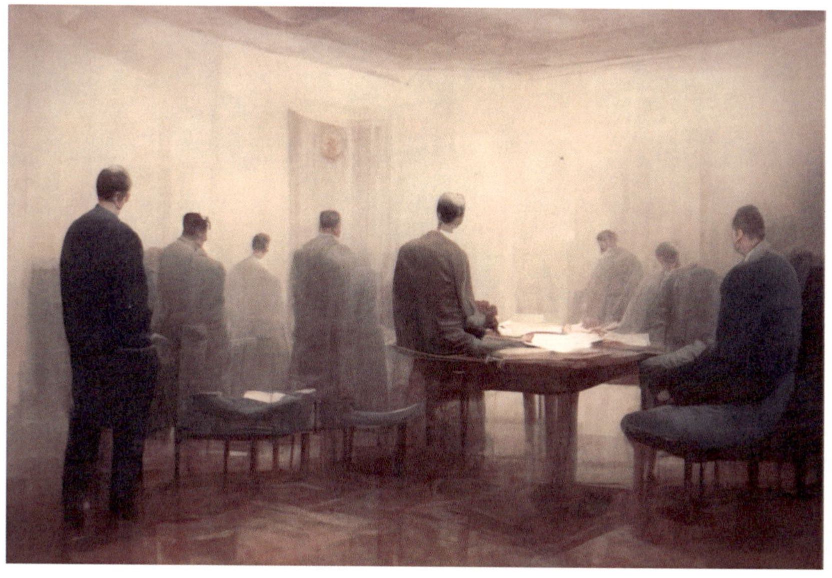

Midjourney ignored the “nine” in the prompt. It doesn’t count very well. It’s 1, 2, or a lot.

WAS IT A CAR OR A CAT I SAW?

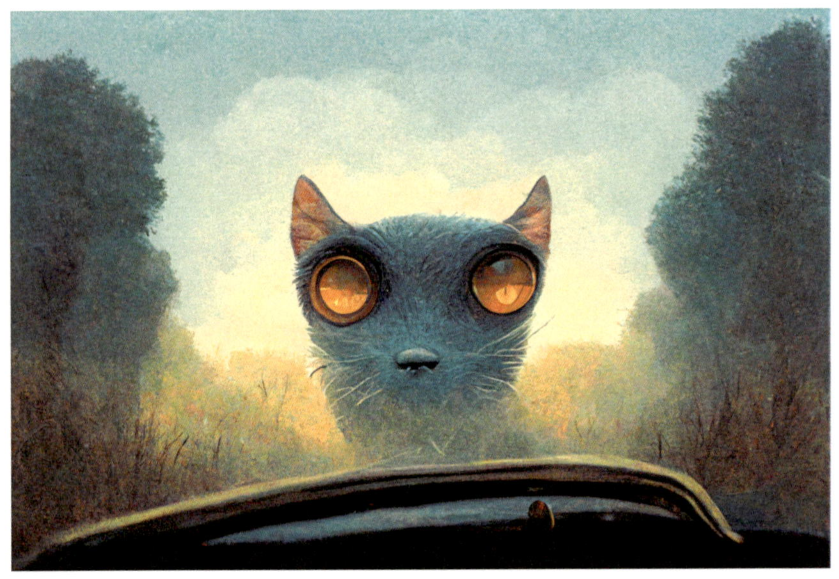

Whatever it was, its eyes looked like headlights!

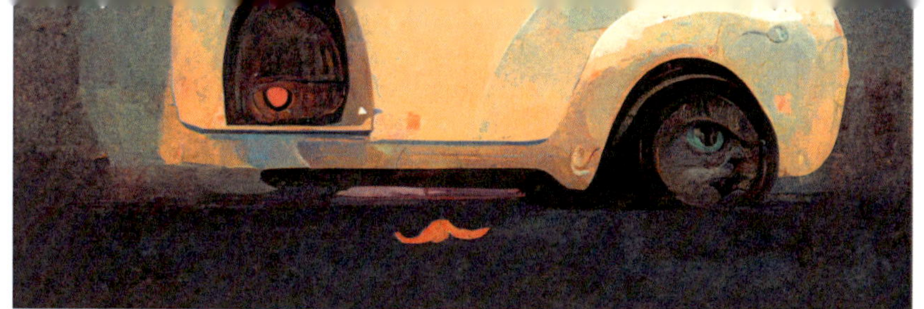

Midjourney was not sure whether it was drawing a car or a cat. There is a car shape, but it has cat ears, and an eye where one of the wheels go.

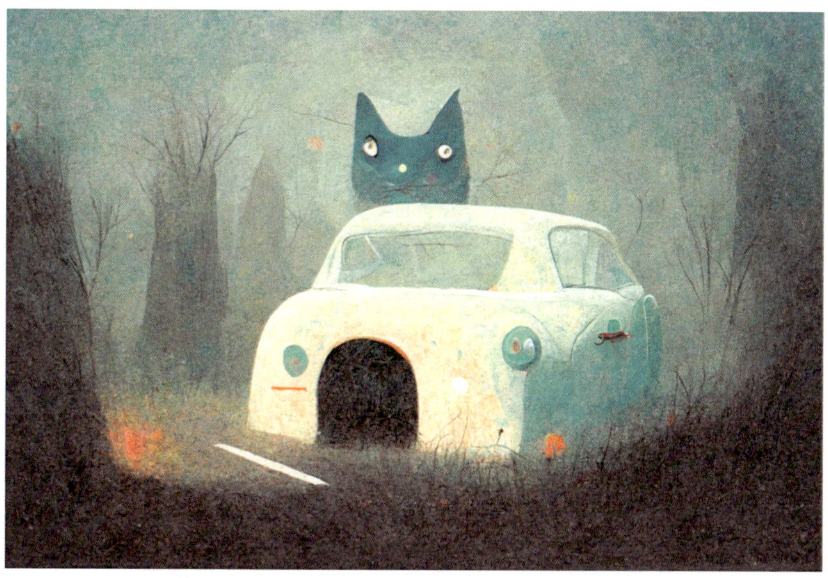

A spooky-cute illustration that captures the car/cat conundrum, Studio Ghibli style.

NO CAB, NO TUNA, A NUT ON BACON

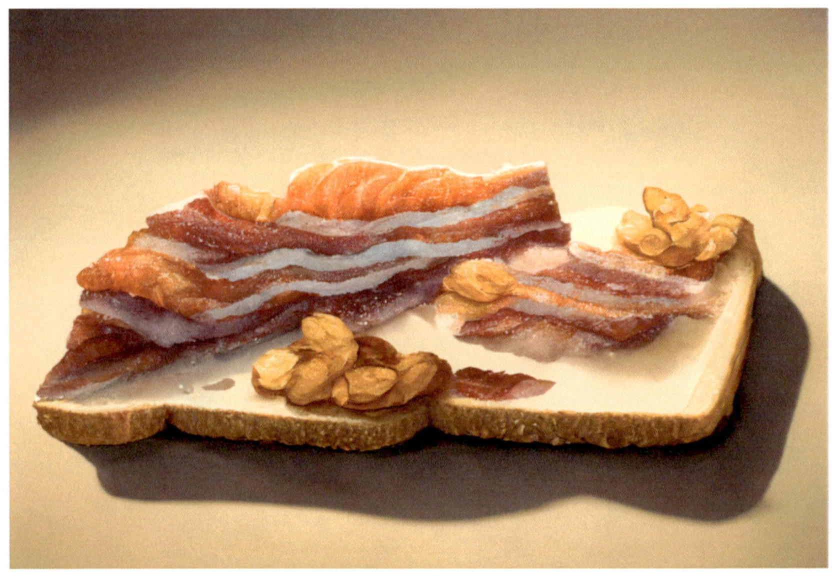

Midjourney AI wanted to treat this palindrome as a sandwich recipe. Nuts and bacon sandwich on white bread, hold the cab, hold the tuna.

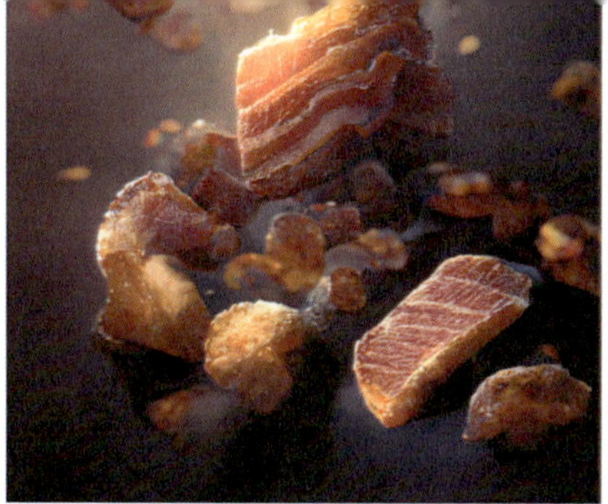

This is in the style of V-ray. V-ray is graphical software that can do photorealistic-quality renderings. Its output has a style and look which MidJourney has learned from examples in its training set.

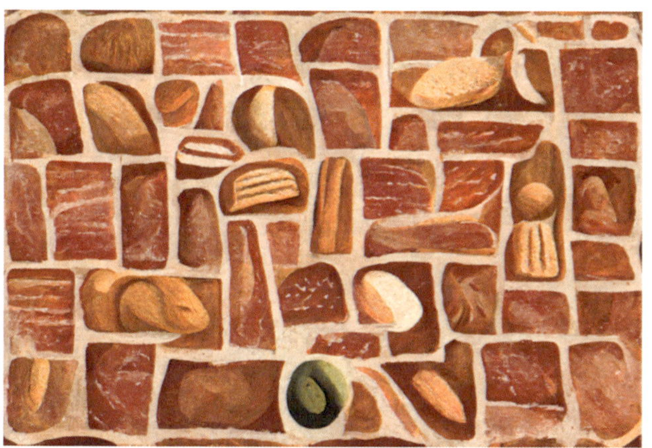

I asked for "No Cab, no Tuna, a Nut on Bacon" as a repeating texture. The result looks like a raw bacon and nuts sampler box. The perfect gift for someone on a low-carb diet?

NO LEMON, NO MELON

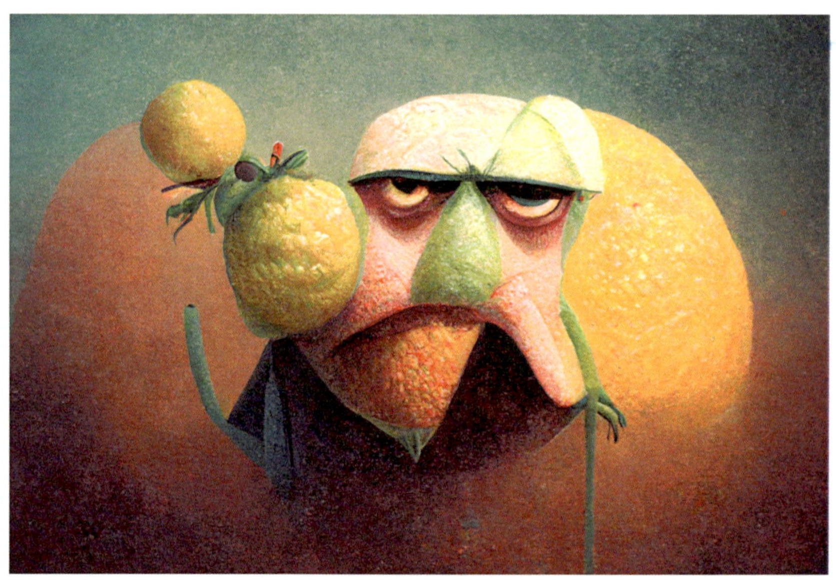

Definitely not a lemon. Definitely not a melon.

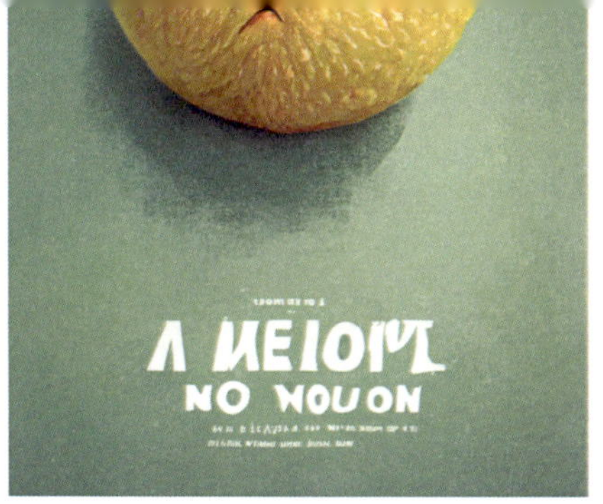

This illustration was in a tall format like a movie poster. The AI added nonsense “words” at the bottom as a graphic element to complete the poster look.

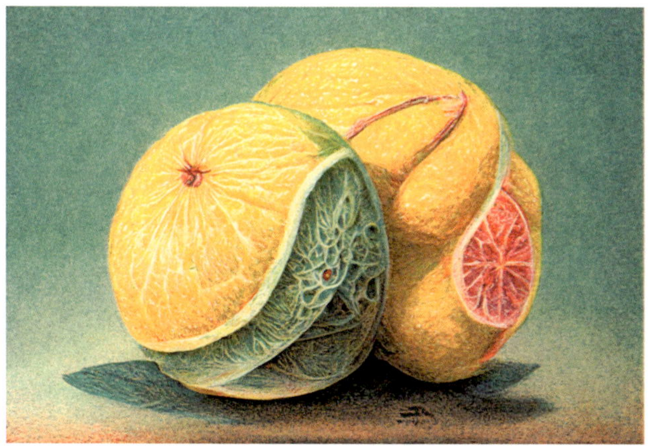

Science isn’t about why, its about why not. Presenting, the Melmon!

A LOT NOT NEW I SAW, AS I WENT ON TO LA

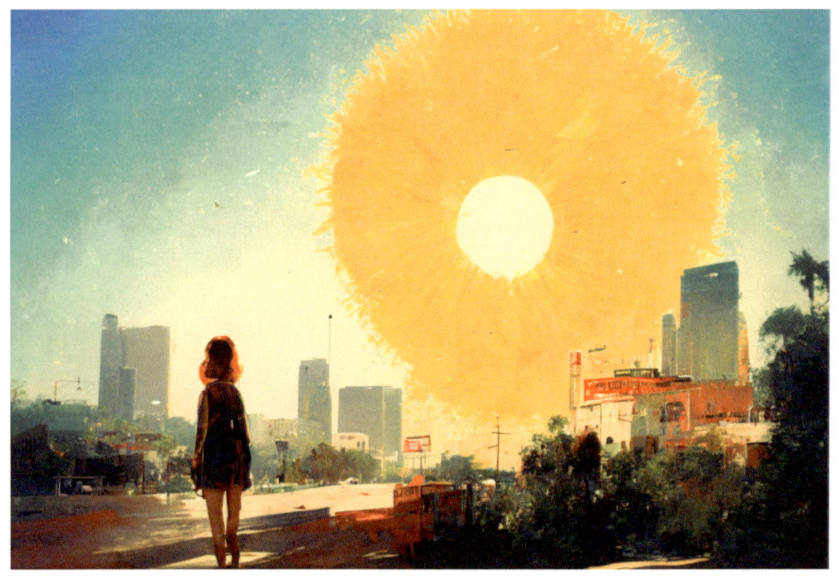

California dreaming, 1960's.

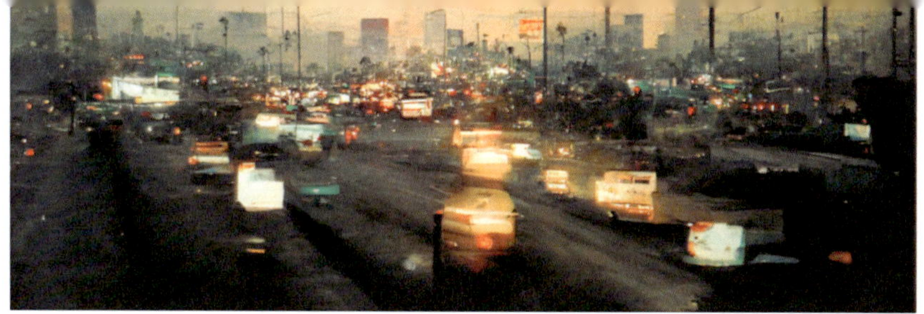

Nothing new here, if you have ever commuted in the LA metro area. Midjourney rendered it like a photograph.

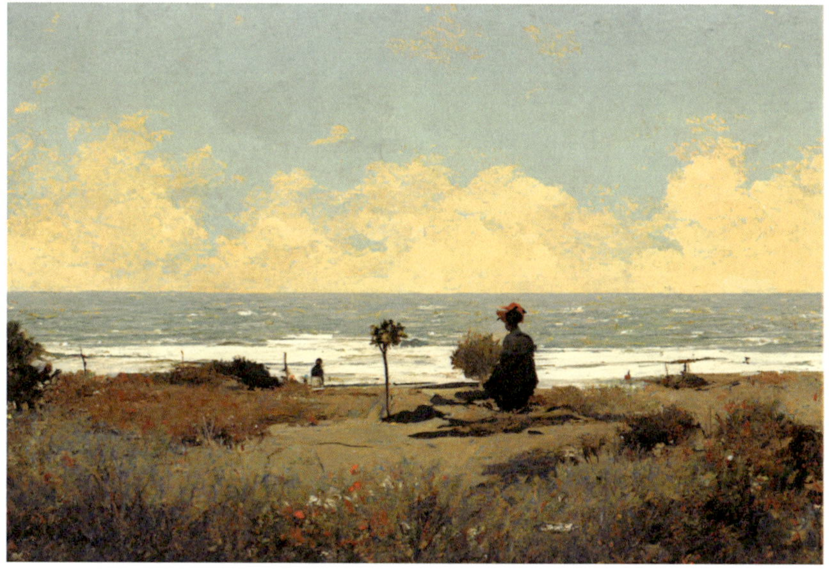

Just west of the sleepy California pueblo of Los Angeles. A painterly interpretation in an old California landscape style.

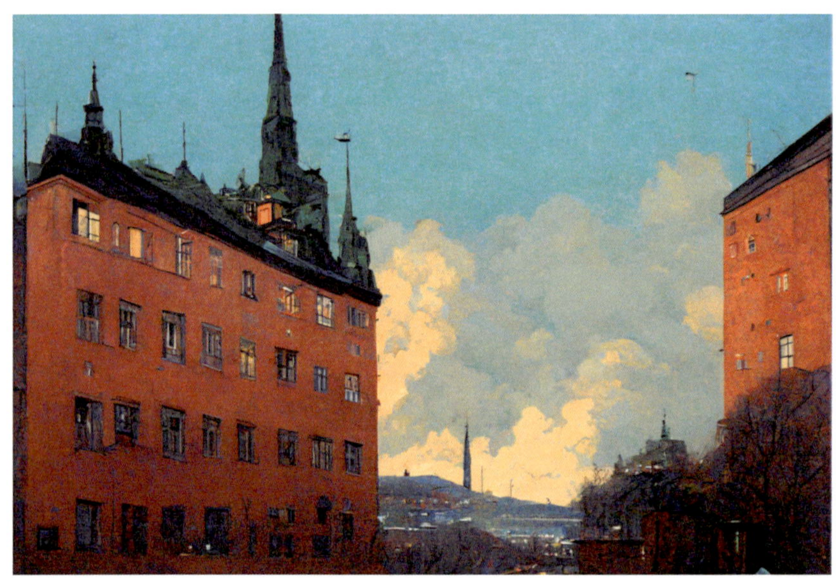

Beautiful, cool winter light.

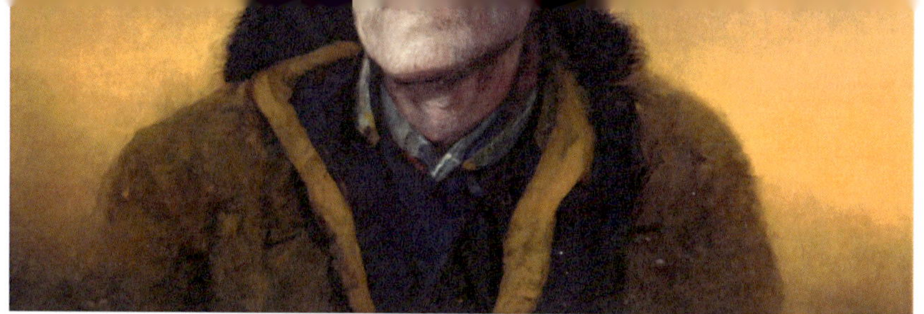

I added James Olson, an actor, to the prompt to help Midjourney draw a human-looking face instead of its usual a nightmarish monstrosity. Tricks like that help.

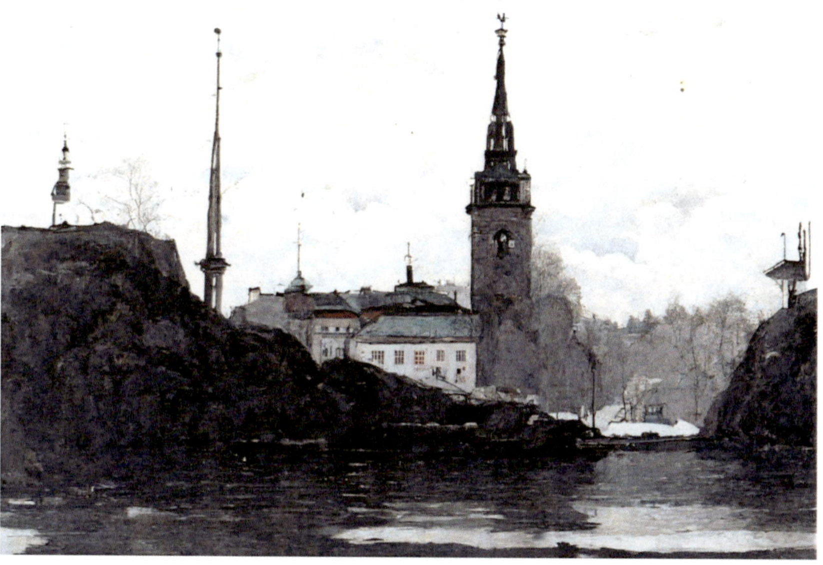

Maybe Paulus Lutheran church in Oslo? But the AI decided to draw it near the water.

ON A CLOVER, IF ALIVE, ERUPTS A VAST, PURE EVIL; A FIRE VOLCANO

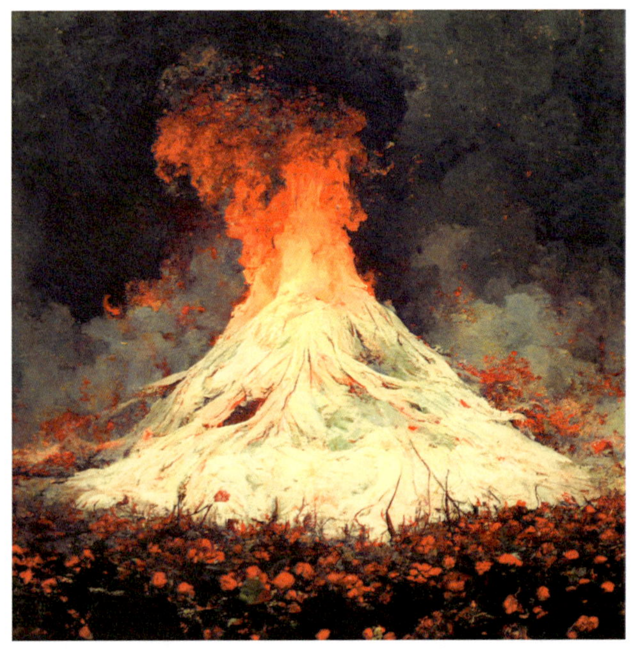

Fire Volcano made of evil white fat erupting from a field of blood-red clover. MidJourney was disgustingly literal in this illustration.

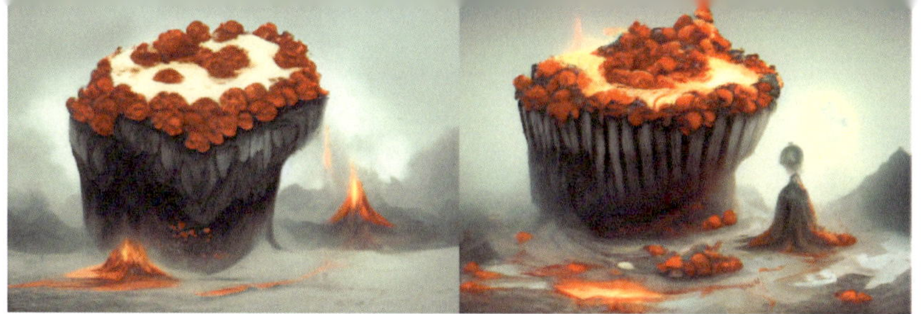

What if the fiery evil was a sinfully fattening cake? Here are some options the AI came up with.

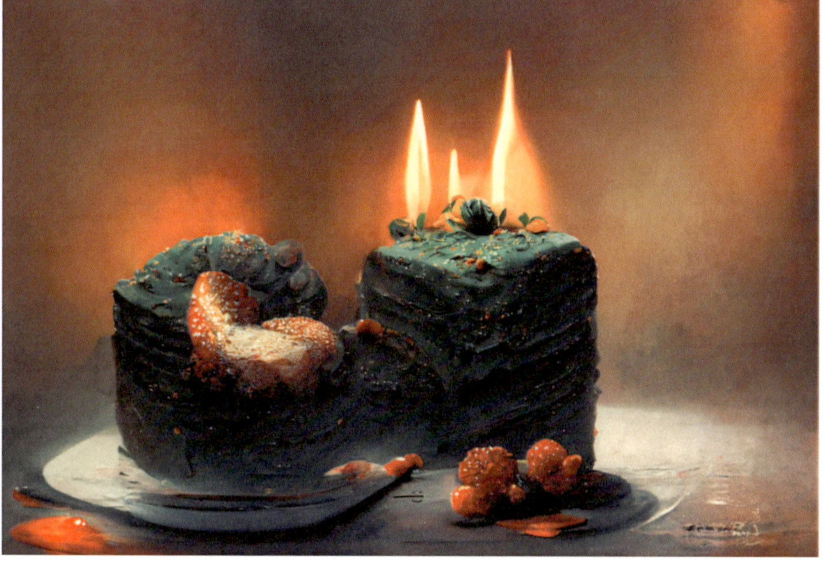

What if the cake was made with extra evil. On fire!

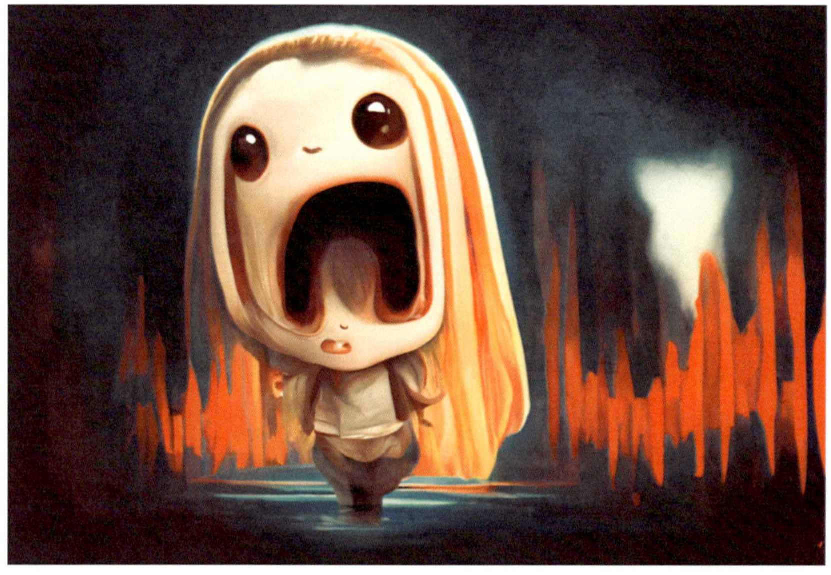

The red in the background reminds me of an EKG printout.

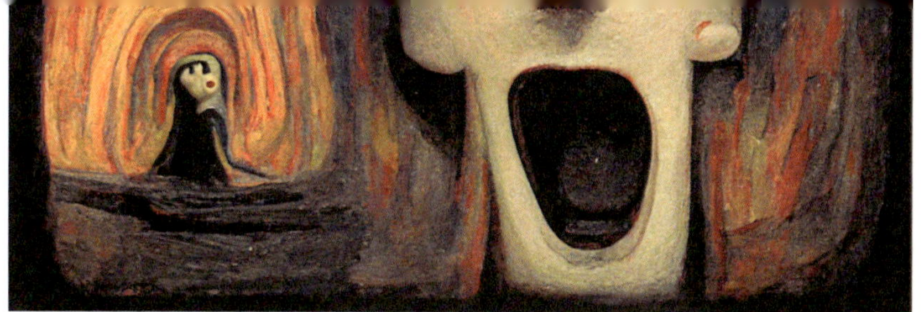

I added "The Scream by Edvard Munch" to the prompt for this series. It gave wide open mouths and colorful lines. Style for this image was "claymation"

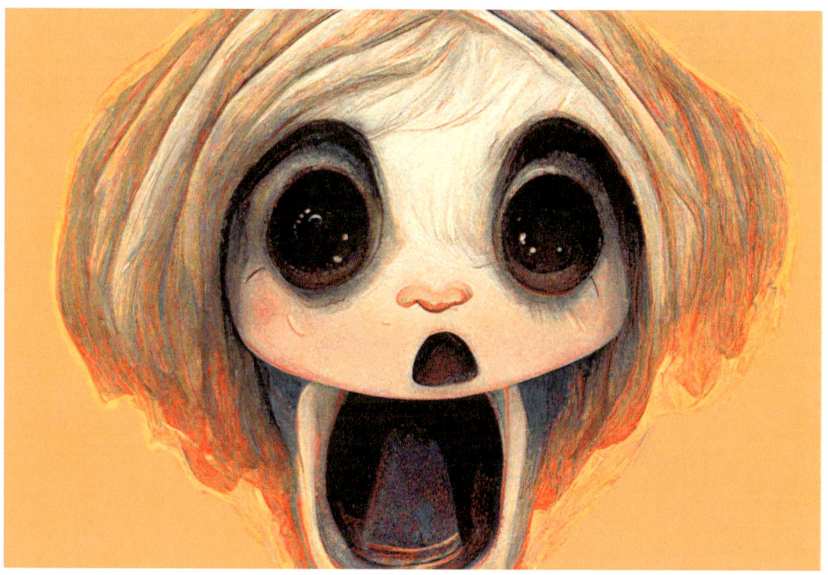

Pit panic—cute edition.

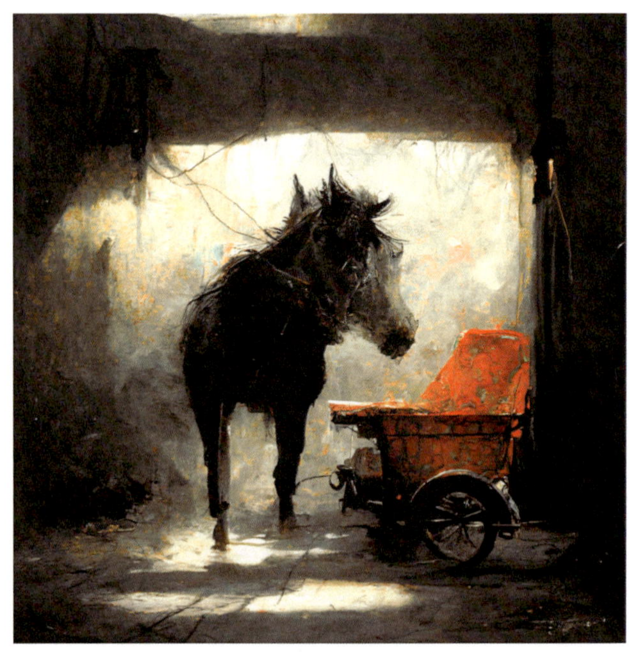

Added “dramatic lighting” and “colorful charcoal” to the base prompt. Best of many. Obsession has its rewards.

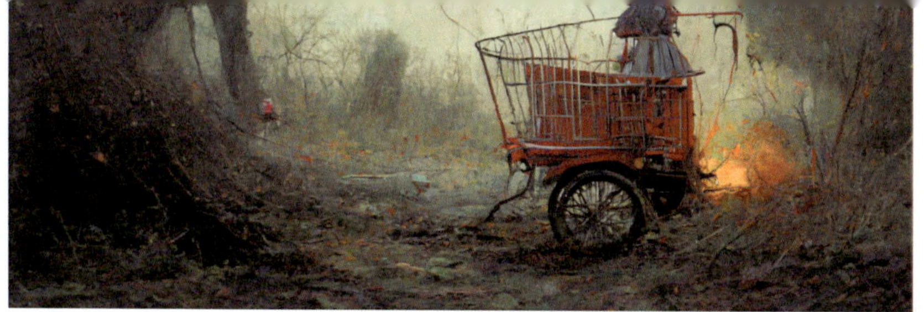

A dark unicorn. The surreal quality of a nightmare. Is the girl really standing in a red Target shopping cart?

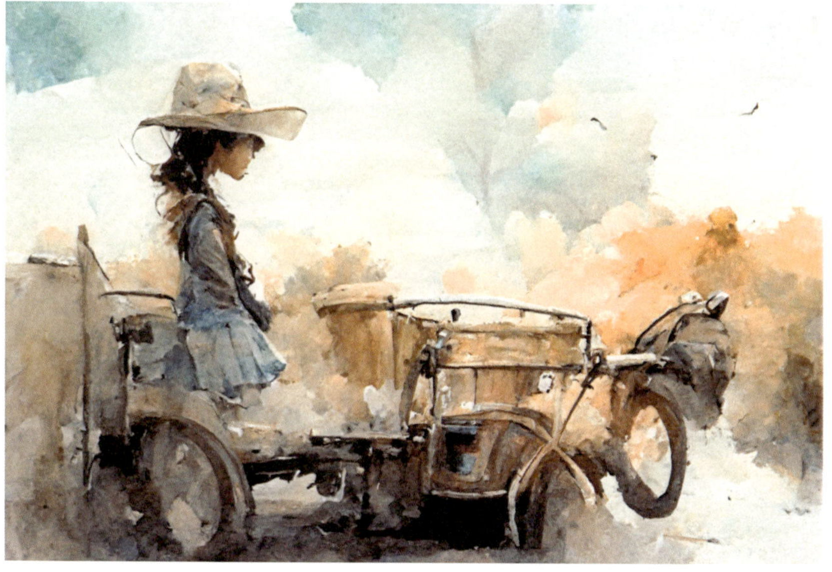

Suggested “cowboy hat” and a watercolor style to nudge Midjourney out of its dark dreaming. Go West AI. Go West.

RATS LIVE ON NO EVIL STAR

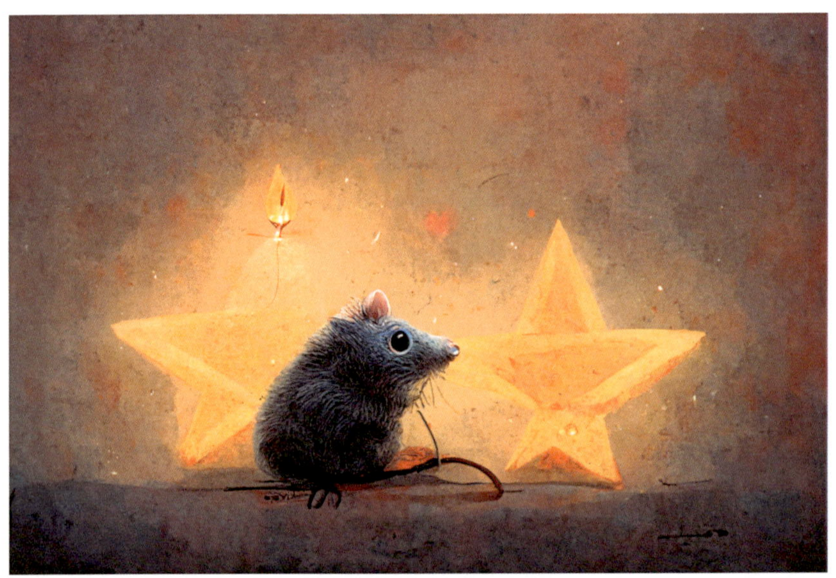

Asked for a cute rat. My wish was granted.

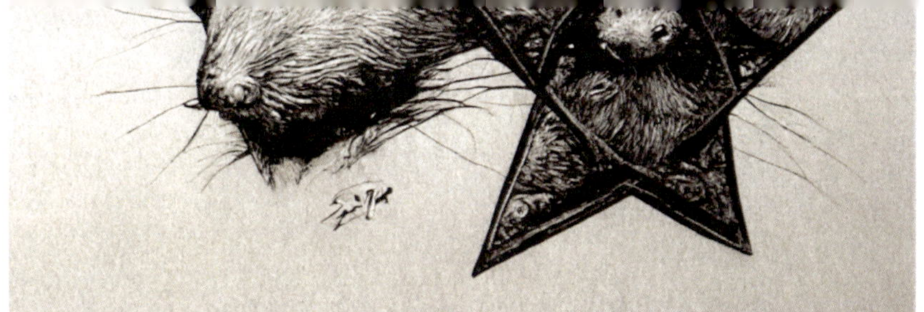

Not so cute, but a very interesting example of detailed pencil-style output.

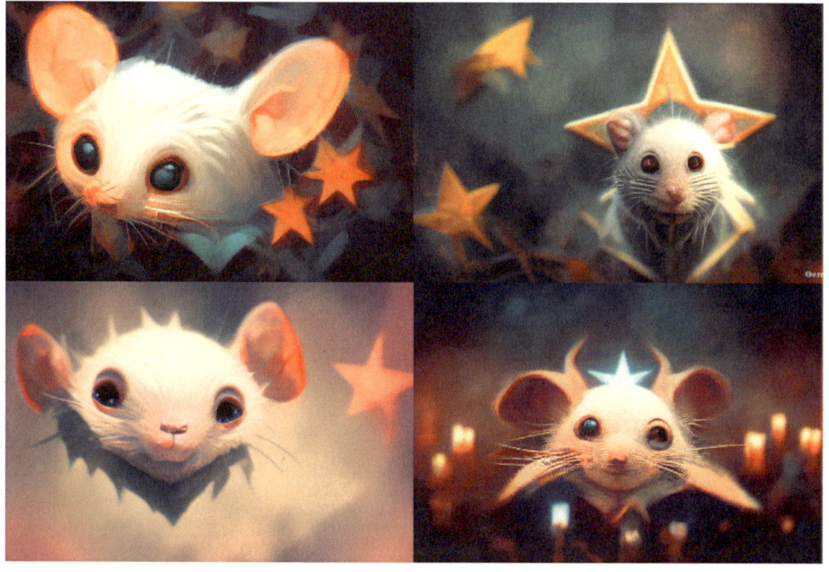

More cute rat concepts. When you get output like this it feels like striking gold. You know that you will be able to develop something. Other times you just get a twisted mess.

A SANTA LIVED AS A DEVIL AT NASA

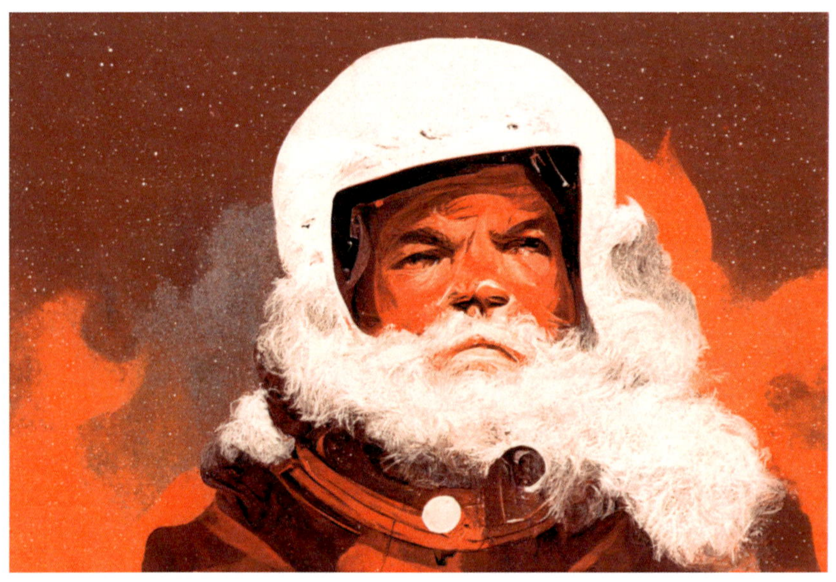

What do you want to be when you grow up? A Santa devil astronaut explorer? Epic career choice!

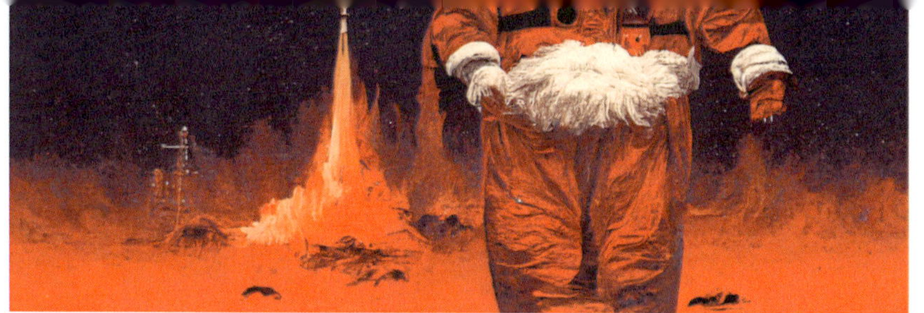

Space Santa with a retro Sci-fi vibe.

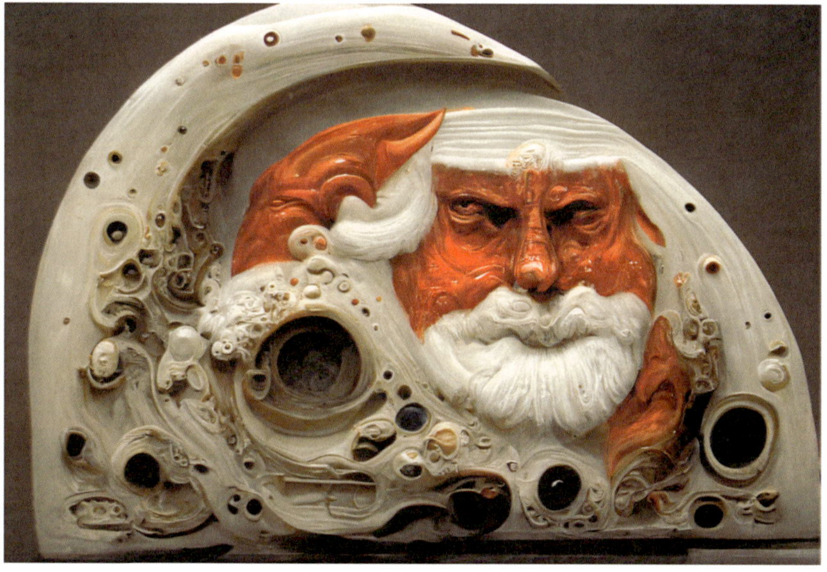

Here is the palindrome prompt interpreted as a ceramic. Happy discoveries like this are one of the best things about exploring AI image generation.

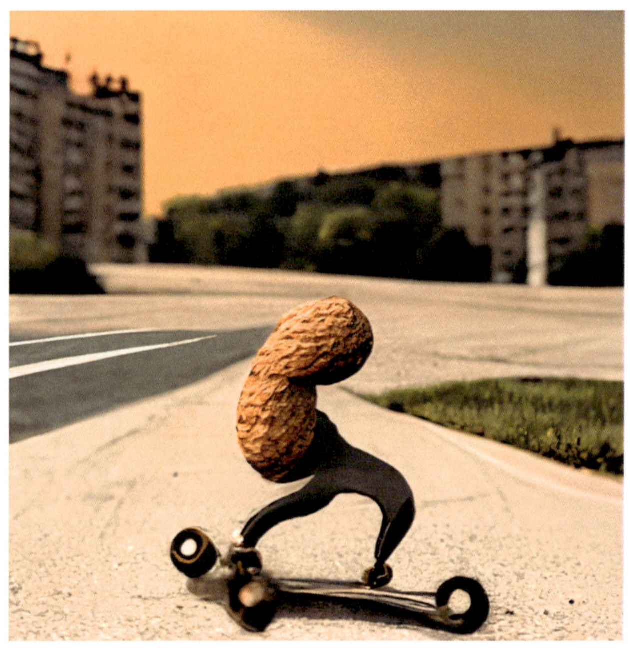

Stunt nut carving a gnarly turn on a skateboard.

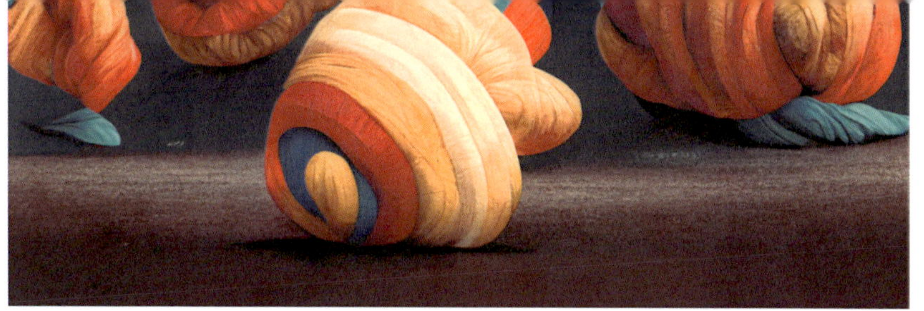

Circus almonds performing stunts on stage.

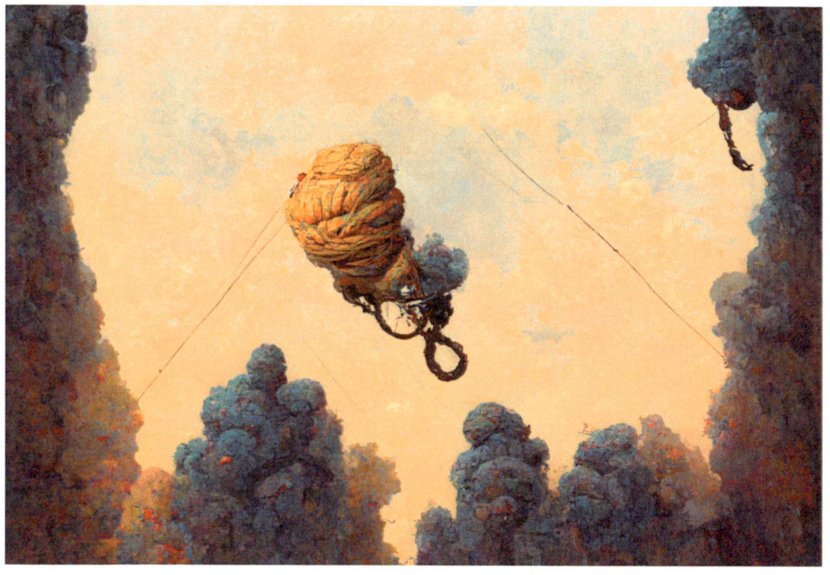

Up and away! A stunt nut sails off into a painterly sky.

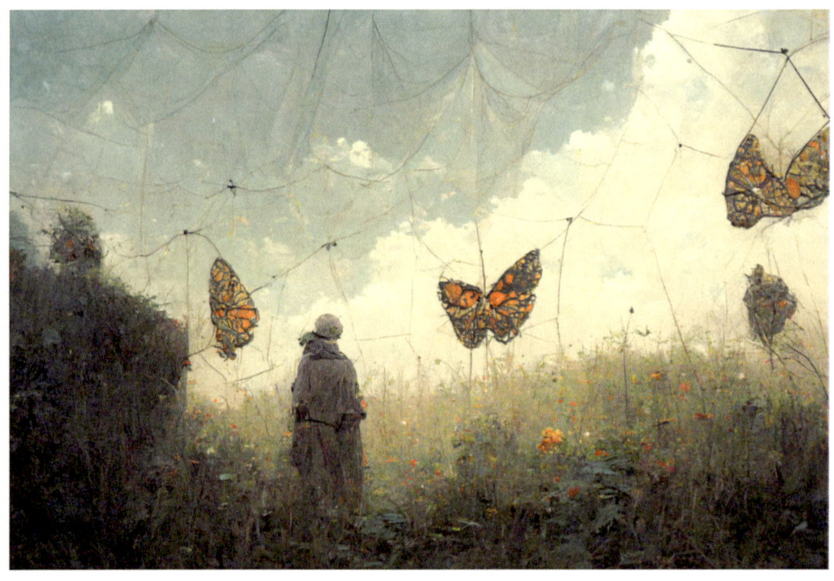

This was a challenging prompt for Midjourney. It took many tries and variations to get a net with more than one creature.

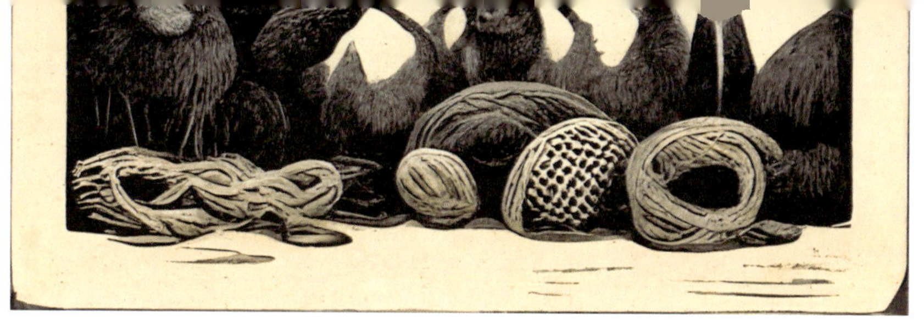

The fox does not look happy about being slammed. Notice the netting materials at the bottom.

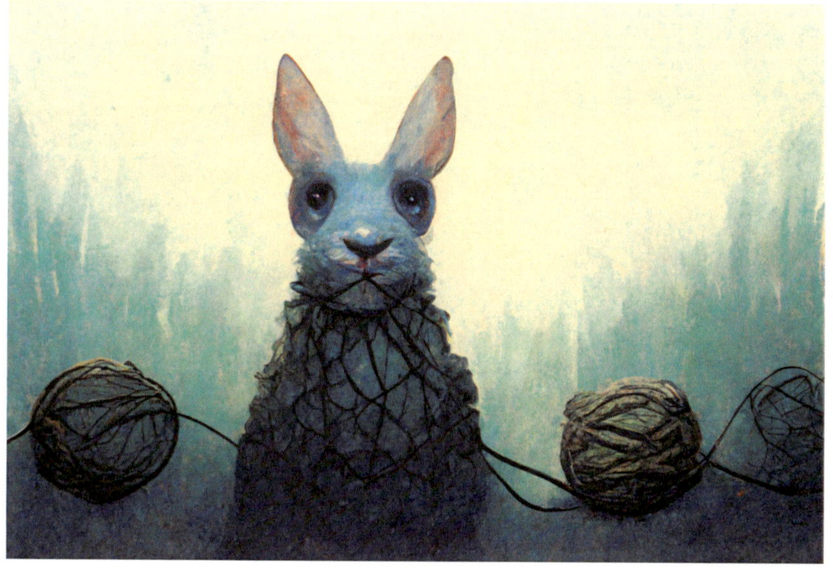

One sad bunny slammed in a net.

UFO TOFU

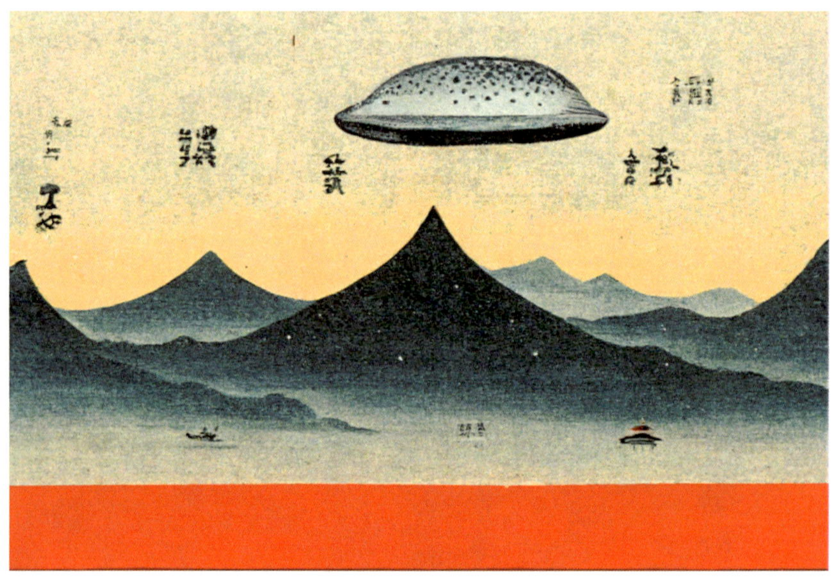

Tofu UFO in the style of Hiroshige.

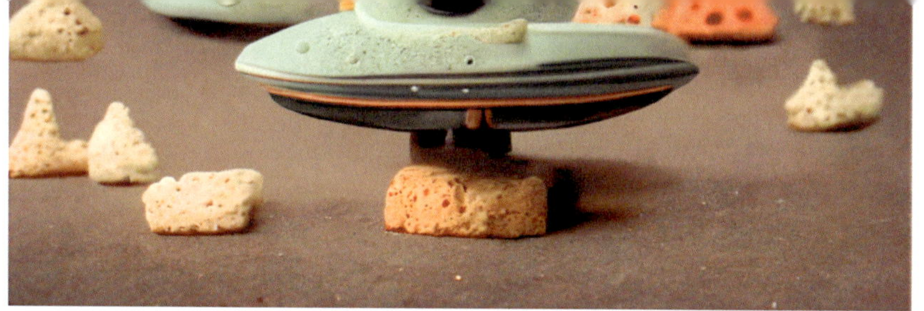

UFO tofu, claymation style. Midjourney draws objects touching the ground for support when it makes claymation images.

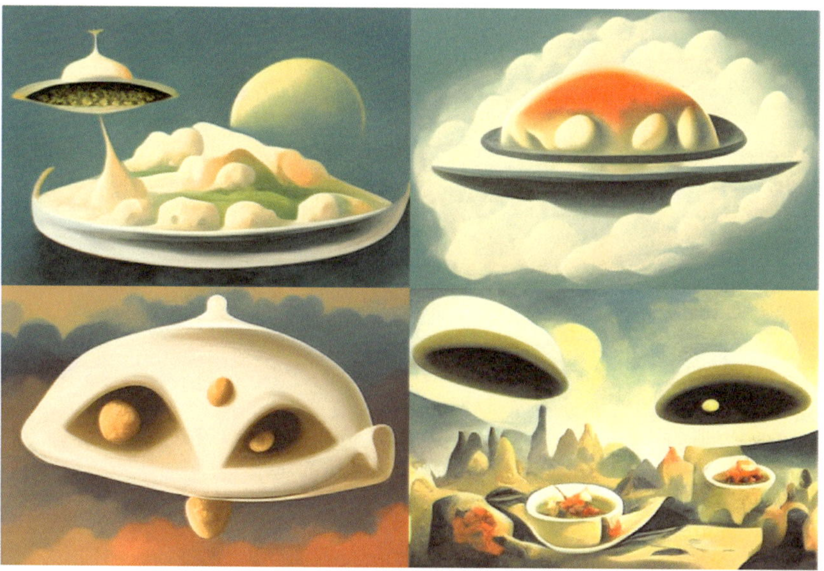

Here are some concepts Midjourney produced for the UFO tofu prompt.

A TOYOTA. RACE FAST, SAFE CAR. A TOYOTA

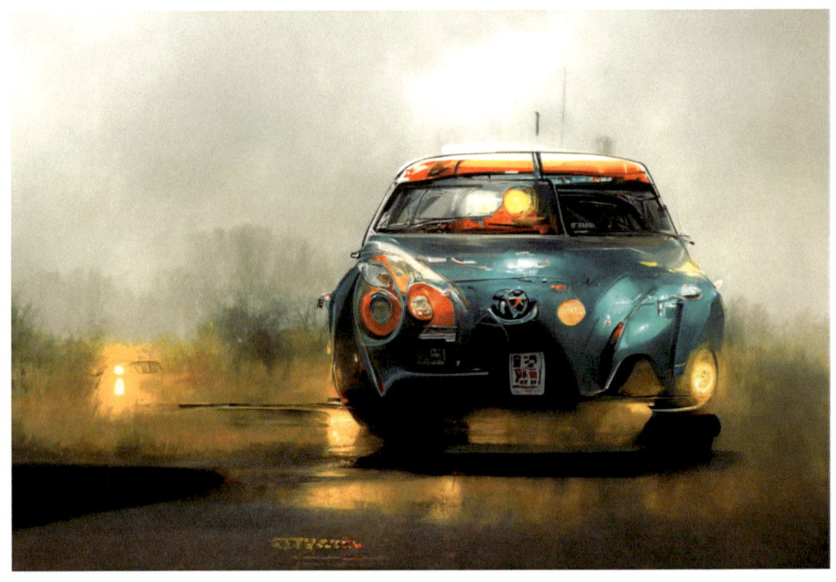

A beautiful, fast, safe Toyota on a rainy afternoon. The fog and golden light on the pavement make the image stand out.

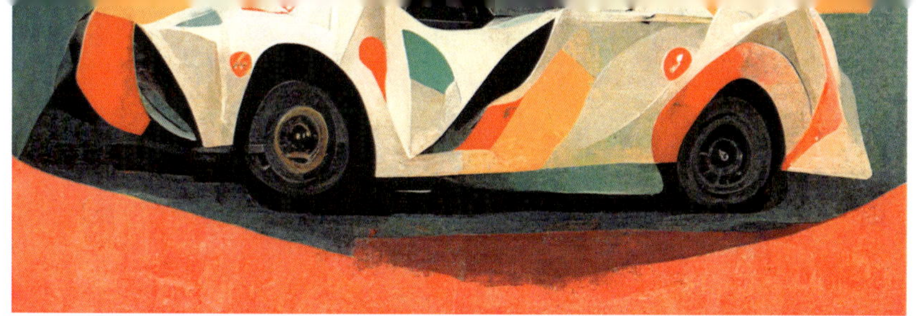

Car courtesy of Toyota. Style courtesy of Picasso.

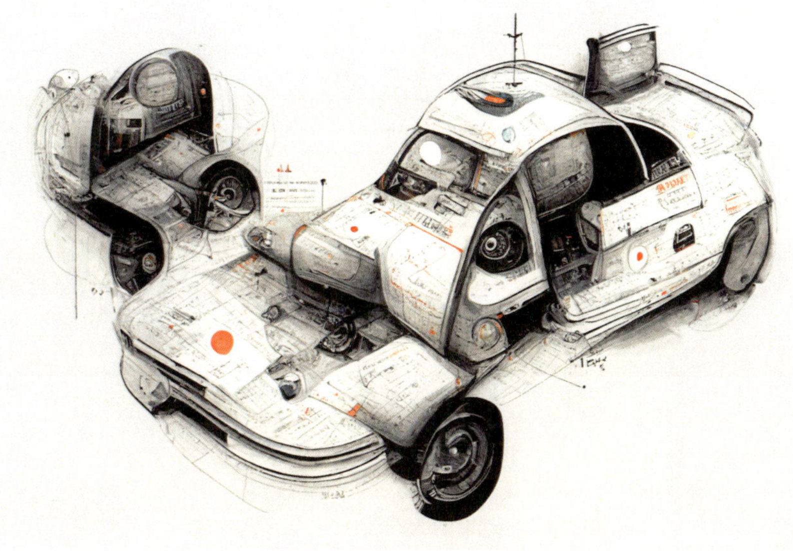

I added “blueprint, diagram, detailed technical drawing” to the base prompt to get some variety. I didn’t expect the AI to cover the car with them

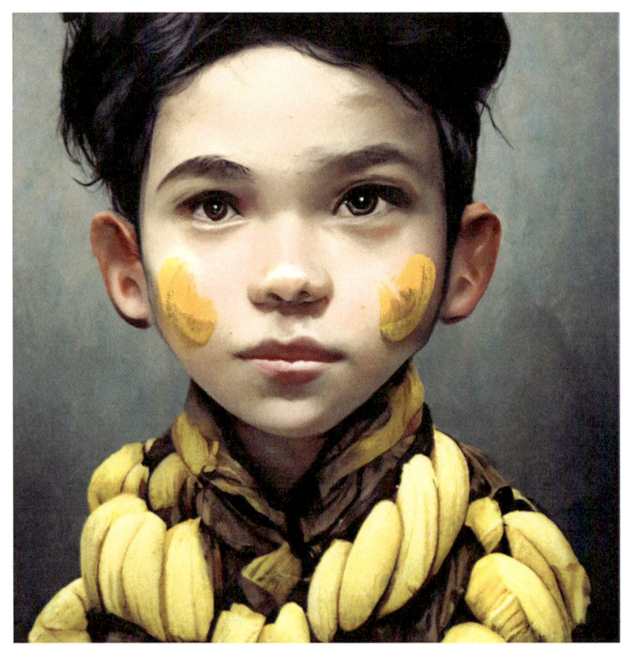

Banana boy wearing a classic banana scarf.

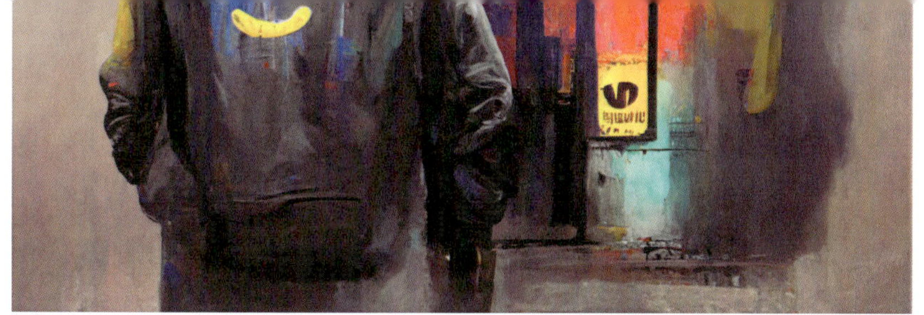

A more urban banana boy look. AI is already being used for fashion design. Get ready for a bold, colorful future.

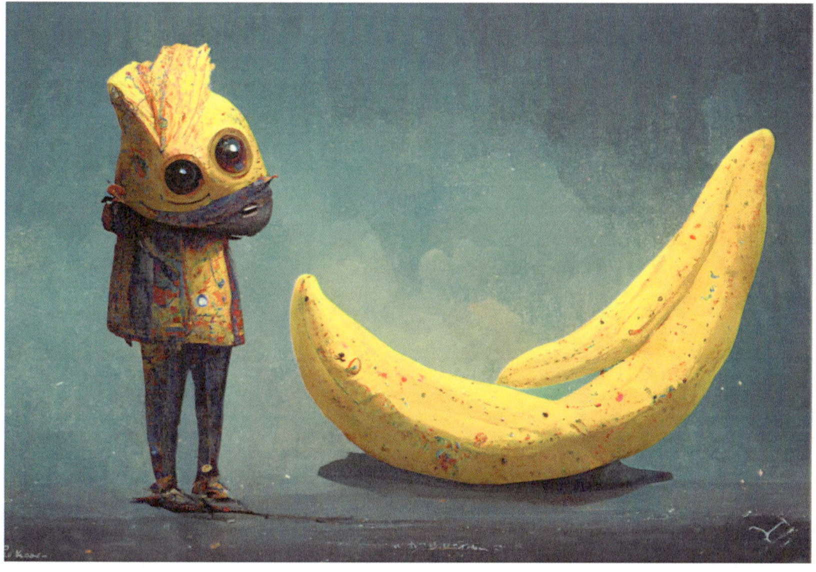

Banana boy hanging out with a bunch of his friends

BLOOPERS

Many of the illustrations in this book required dozens or even hundreds of tries to obtain the final images. There were hilariously flawed images, many near-misses, and some complete train wrecks. Here are some of the best of the worst.

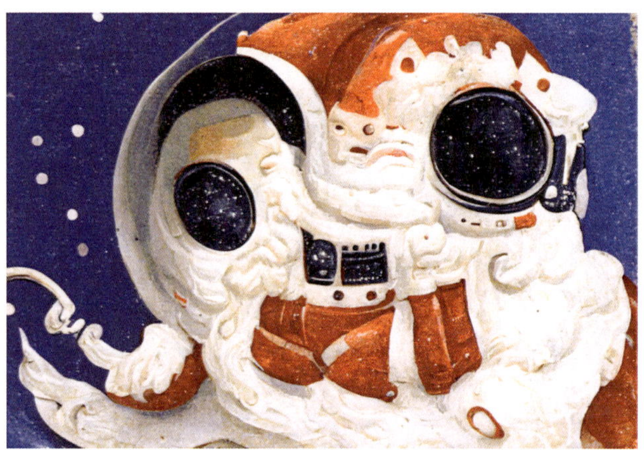

A Santa Lived as a Devil At NASA (ceramic nightmare style).

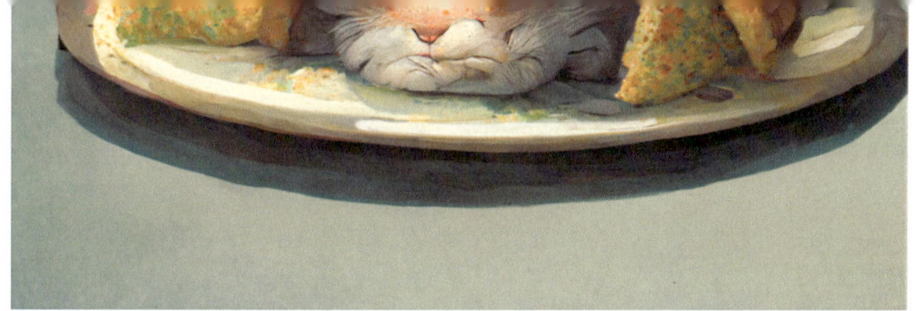

Taco Cat as a main course. Ewww.

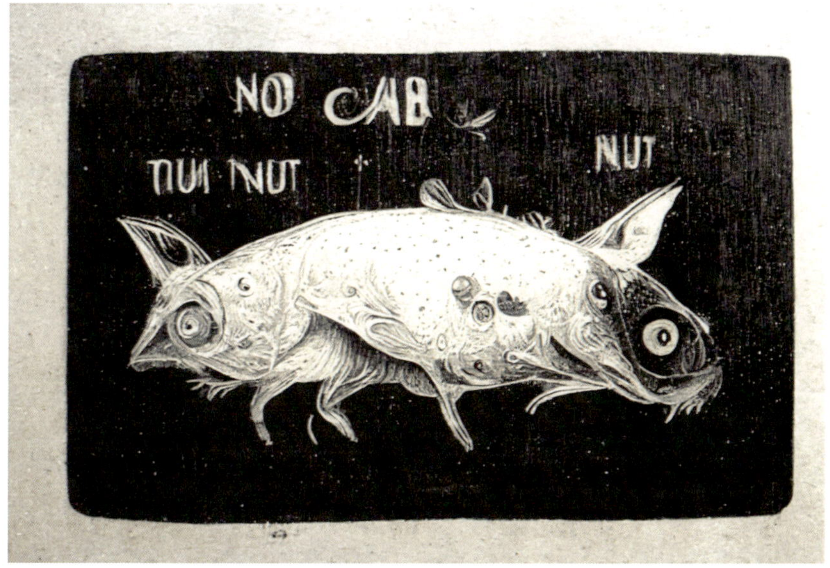

No Cab No Tuna, a Nut on Bacon. What?

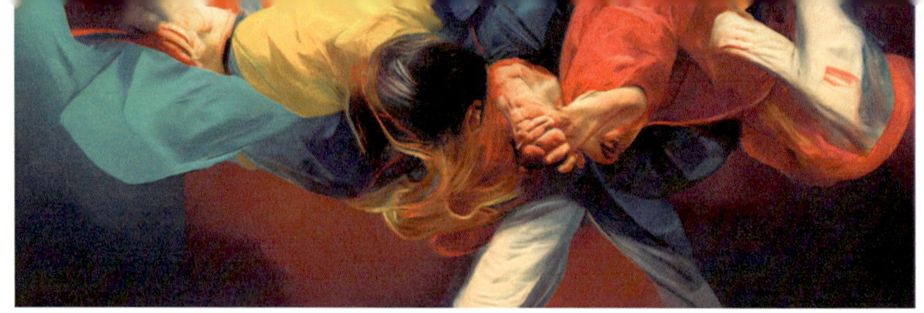

Jujitsu gone wrong.

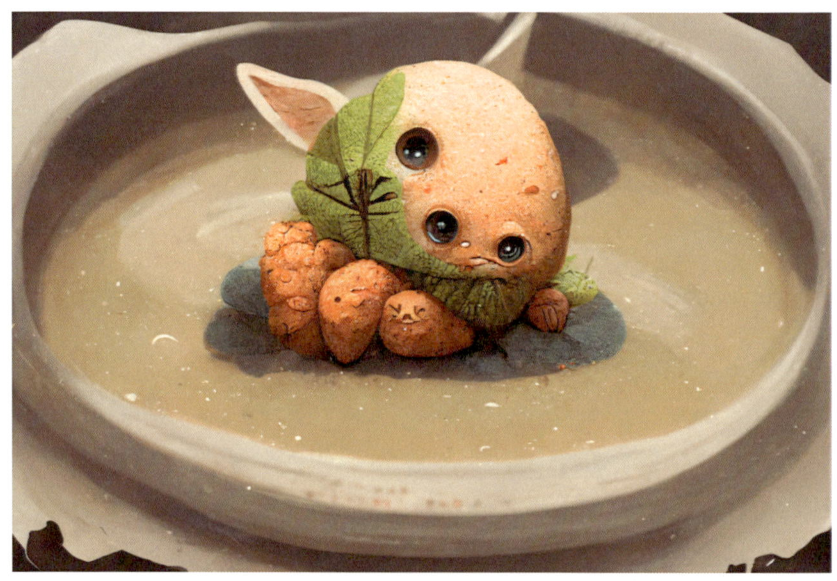

Doomed yams in a balsamic reduction with baby…beet leaves.

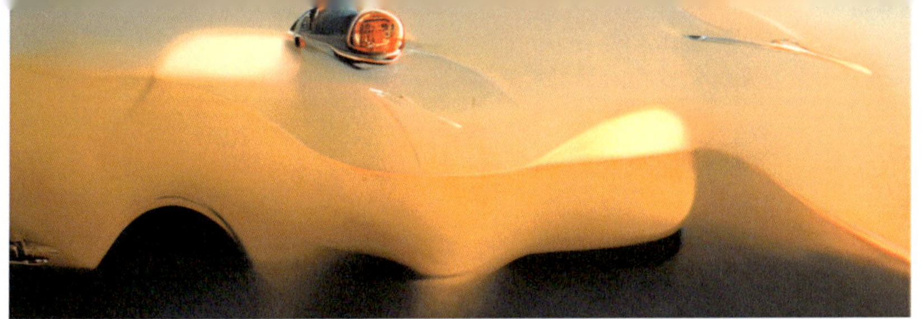

Toyota. Race fast, Safe Car. Um, Toyota?

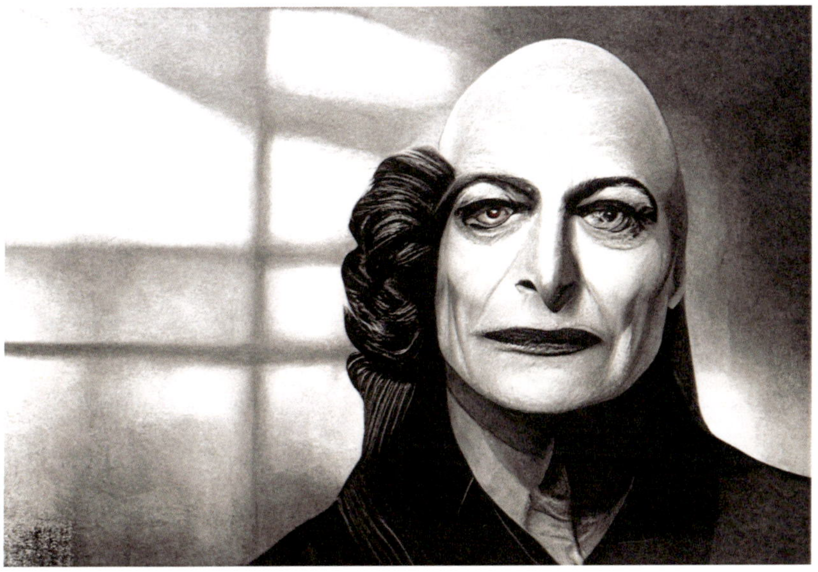

Madam, I'm Adam. I'm here to retrieve my hair.

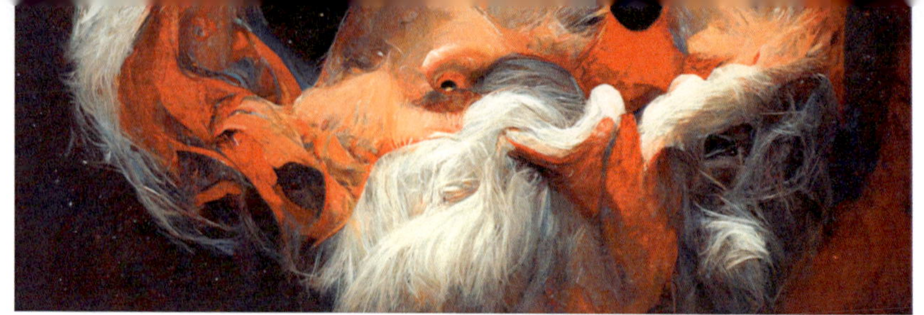

NASA Santa as co-joined twins.

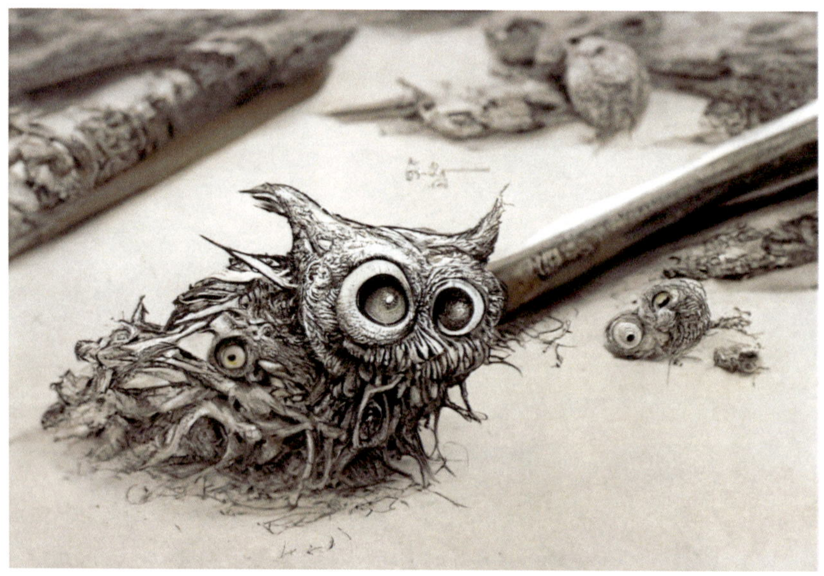

Mr. Owl, gone awry.

James Lawson has been making quirky digital art for years and years. He has been combining words into silly sentences for even longer.

He has way too many hobbies and loves to learn new things.

Sometimes, James helps Anthea Sharp at Fiddlehead Press. Other times, he hinders and distracts her.

It's a happy life.

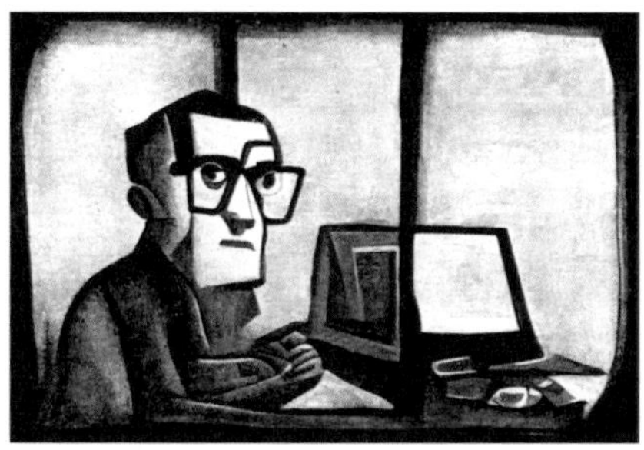

www.ingramcontent.com/pod-product-compliance
Lightning Source LLC
Chambersburg PA
CBRC091249050726
47599CB00013B/1036

* 9 7 8 1 6 8 0 1 3 1 5 5 0 *